Penguin Books

The Loch Ness Story

Nicholas Witchell was born in Shropshire, England, in 1953. He was educated at Epsom College and is currently finishing a law degree at Leeds University where he served as the full-time editor of the city's student newspaper. His interest and involvement in the Loch Ness mystery dates back to his early teens. Since then he has spent many months at the loch researching the history of the affair and taking part in the various investigation activities.

The
Loch Ness Story

Nicholas Witchell

Penguin Books

Penguin Books Ltd,
Harmondsworth, Middlesex, England
Penguin Books Inc.,
7110 Ambassador Road, Baltimore, Maryland 21207, U.S.A.
Penguin Books Australia Ltd,
Ringwood, Victoria, Australia
Penguin Books Canada Ltd,
41 Steelcase Road West, Markham, Ontario, Canada
Penguin Books (N.Z.) Ltd,
182–190 Wairau Road, Auckland 10, New Zealand

First published by Terence Dalton Ltd 1974
This revised edition published in Penguin Books 1975

Copyright © Nicholas Witchell, 1974, 1975

Made and printed in Great Britain by
Cox & Wyman Ltd, London, Reading and Fakenham
Set in Intertype Times

Contents

Author's Preface

to the Penguin Edition

This paperback edition of *The Loch Ness Story* is being rushed out in the autumn of 1975 at a time when the world is about to witness one of the greatest and most dramatic discoveries of the twentieth century: the discovery and probable identification of a semi-mythical creature known throughout the world as the 'Monster' of Scotland's Loch Ness.

As the final chapter describes, a set of detailed colour photographs of the head and body of the 'Monster' has been taken by a highly respected American scientific team. They have set the zoological world, and will very shortly set the whole scientific and lay world, ablaze with excitement. After nearly fifty years of legend and mystery, the saga of the Loch Ness 'Monster' is about to end with the addition of a remarkable new (or possibly very ancient) species to the world's animal kingdom.

It is my hope that this unique and complete history of the Loch Ness phenomenon may provide an insight into the intriguing manner in which a periodically amused but basically indifferent twentieth-century society, and a frenziedly evasive scientific community, has reacted to a mystery which they have been unable, for nearly half a century, to categorize.

First on the list of people to whom I owe most sincere thanks is an outstanding predecessor in the Loch Ness litany, Constance Whyte, author in 1957 of *More Than a Legend – The Story of the Loch Ness Monster*, the first post-war rallying cry and the seminal point for the modern 'monster-hunt'. Her unique archives have been the factual source of much of this book, whilst her encouragement and advice have both abetted and corrected, to a considerable degree, the author.

Outstanding also among those who have assisted me have been Wing-Commander and Mrs Basil Cary, whose great hospitality has made the months I have spent at Loch Ness such a great pleasure. Of immense value in filling in detail and placing events in perspective has been the help of Tim Dinsdale, Dr Robert Rines, Alan Jones, Professor Roy Mackal, F. W. Holiday, David James, Alex Campbell, Captain James Fraser, Peter and Pauline Hodge, and Lorn MacIntyre of the Department of Gaelic History at the University of Glasgow.

Impersonal though lists are, I can find no other way of recording my thanks to the following for their help: Holly Arnold, Hugh Ayton, Lady Maud Baillie, Barbara Baker, Eveline Barron, Bob Boddey, the late Mrs Margaret Cameron, Father Aloysius Carruth, Dr D. J. Creasey, Peter Davies, Dorothy Fraser, Rip Hepple, Steve Hurst, Richard and Phyllis Jenkyns, Ted Lafleur, Elizabeth MacGruer, William Mackay, Peter Macnab, Clive Main, Ron Mercer, Sir Brian Mountain, Richard Need, Ivor Newby, William Owen, Dick Raynor, Graham Snape, Murray Stewart, Thelma Warden, Gwen Wilson, Mike Wolf, Charles Wykoff, and the staff of the many picture libraries and newspaper offices I have consulted. Very special thanks too to Mr Gerald Durrell for his splendid foreword, to Terence Dalton and John Venmore Rowland at Terence Dalton Ltd, and to all the copyright-holders of the illustrations.

I concluded the hardback edition of this book with a quotation from the poet Byron. There seems to be no more appropriate note with which to end the Preface to this new and revised edition: 'Tis strange – but true; for truth is always strange – stranger than fiction.'

Nicholas Witchell

Leeds, 18 September 1975

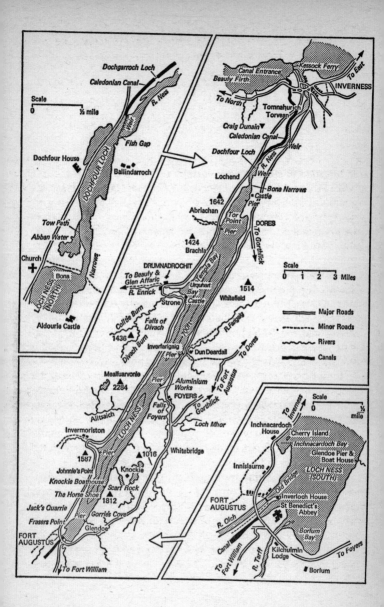

Foreword to the First Edition

by Gerald Durrell

It has always seemed very curious to me that anybody faced with reasonably good evidence (supplied by witnesses of guaranteed probity and sobriety) as to the possible existence of a creature as yet unknown to science, should not throw up their hands in delight at even the faintest chance of such a windfall in this shrinking world. Unfortunately, as Mr Witchell's book shows, the opposite is generally the case. Man, whose intelligence you had no cause to doubt, suddenly leaves you bereft of speech at the lengths to which he will go to prove that nothing new can exist under the stars. It was Cuvier who produced the arrogant statement that there were no new large animals to be discovered for, as he pointed out, he knew them all. Since that date, there has been an endless succession of equally arrogant people who adopt the same blinkered attitude.

In this book Mr Witchell has collected and clearly set out the saga of the Loch Ness Monster and it makes fascinating reading; but, as he rightly points out, 'It is a puzzling reflection on our purportedly intelligent, rational society that the testimony of so many reliable witnesses, often offered under oath, should have been considered inadequate as proof that there is something unknown in Loch Ness.'

I am not suggesting for a moment that one accepts the existence of an unknown creature without sifting the evidence with great care, but what I am advocating – and surely this should not be too much to hope for in scientific circles – is a reasonably open mind. There are after all sufficiently strange things in the world which we now accept but which at one time were considered very dubious indeed. Think of the courage it must have

taken to set out to describe to the scientific fraternity the first
duck-billed platypus.

So many people state that a prehistoric monster (that loose
generic term so beloved of the press) could not exist today. Yet
they have only to travel to New Zealand, where they will find
the Tuatara (Sphenodon punctatus) which has, with scant lack
of consideration for science, come down from the pleistocene
age unchanged; and this is not the only survivor, as Mr Witchell
points out. The coelacanth could not be more of a prehistoric
creature if it tried.

In these pages we have the extraordinary cross section of
observant intelligent witnesses who are above reproach being
virtually told by the scientists that they are either drunk, insane,
hoaxers or partially blind and all definitely mentally retarded.
Faced with evidence that seems to me incontrovertible, that
something large and unknown exists in the Loch, the scientific
fraternity nervously takes refuge behind a barricade of ripples,
leaping salmon, shadows, dead stags, logs of wood, branches,
and what must surely be the most agile and acrobatic strings of
otters ever seen, rather than admit that there is something large,
strange and unknown to science in the cold waters of the
loch.

It seems incredible also that all the research to date has had to
be done virtually on a shoe string by dedicated amateurs who,
when they were helped at all, received assistance from places
like America while receiving precious little but a petulant moue
from the disbelieving ranks of British Science. You would have
thought that even the British Tourist Board could have spent a
little less money in sending mini-kilted young ladies and out-of-
focus coloured pictures of heather around the world, in an attempt to attract tourists to the Highlands, and, instead, back to
the hilt an expedition or a series of expeditions finally to identify the creature or creatures in Loch Ness once and for all.
Surely, even a public relations officer, lowly species of animal
life that it is, could appreciate what an enormous attraction it
would be to prove that Scotland supports a living group of
Palaeosaurus. Mr Philip Stalker, writing about the Loch Ness
Monster in 1957, pointed out that 'If medical science had

shown as little enterprise and as little courage, in its various fields, as marine zoologists have shown in regard to the Loch Ness animal, the Gold Coast would still be the White Man's Grave, appendicitis would still be a fatal illness and tuberculosis would be killing millions every year in Britain.' It seems to me fair comment.

I hope that this excellent and lucid account might prod the powers-that-be into doing two things. Firstly, giving financial support to an all-out effort to find out exactly what *does* exist in Loch Ness, and secondly (before this is done) to pass some sort of legislation completely protecting whatever it is that may be found from any harm that could come to it. It would be a sad (but perhaps not altogether surprising) comment on human beings if a creature which had come down unchanged and unharmed from prehistory was to be finally exterminated by modern man.

Gerald Durrell, F.I.A.L., M.I.Biol.

Jersey Wildlife Preservation Trust
Jersey
Channel Islands

Chapter One

The Scales in Balance

'Aye, my father saw it, round about the turn of the century' – the old crofter spoke so softly he was barely audible. He hadn't sought an audience but he immediately got one.

His gaze shifted slowly, across the neatly stacked rows of electronic underwater equipment, valued conservatively at $100,000, and out on to the quiescent waters of the great lake below. 'Aye,' he sighed, continuing in the soft Highland brogue and nodding his head gently, 'he was out in the bay there, doing a wee bit of poaching one evening, when the big beast raced by. It very near capsized him.'

The date: June 1975. The last 'Monster' hunt at Loch Ness was about to get under way. Although we had no idea at the time, we were right on the verge of unravelling the final knots of Nature's greatest mystery; the 'Monster' legend was about to be solved conclusively and for all time.

The electronic hardware had been flown in from the States a few days earlier; now, laid out in that shed high above Urquhart Bay, the dulled screens on the big sonar sets, loaned by the U.S. Navy, stared lifelessly at the old man as he listed details we had all heard so many, many times: 'A big beast, black, with a long thin neck and a small head. A huge, bulky body which threw up a disturbance large enough to capsize a rowing boat.' That was it, all right – that was the quarry, the fabled creature whose pedigree spans more than a thousand years, whose possible existence has puzzled and enthralled people from every corner of the world, and whose reputation commands more attention than those of all but a handful of human personalities.

We all felt humble in the presence of that old man, for despite the complexity and ingenuity of twentieth-century science – represented there by the sonar, the navigational device which tuned in to satellite radio waves, and the computer-controlled underwater camera system which would respond automatically to the presence of large, animate objects – despite all this, we knew precious little more about the loch's mystery than had the old man's father, three quarters of a century before.

By the time this book is published, however, we should know a lot more because, by then, an amazing set of close-up colour photographs of one of the animals taken a few days later will have been released for world scrutiny. Even as these words are being written, at the end of September, the pictures, which show the head and body of one of the creatures in clear detail, are being excitedly studied by the top zoologists of Britain and America (for full details of these new pictures see Chapter 9).

The man responsible for these dramatic advances in the 43-year-old hunt for 'Nessie' had been listening attentively to the Highlander tell his tale. Dr Robert Rines, a former Harvard University lecturer and now a leading American patent attorney and President of the privately-run Academy of Applied Science of Boston, Massachusetts, turned and resumed work on the camera which would shortly be lowered into the gloom of Loch Ness to produce the final answers to this greatest of all zoological investigations.

'A small slice of luck, that's all we need,' he muttered, snapping open one of the underwater cameras designed for use by the French marine explorer Jacques Cousteau, 'and then we'll have all the answers.'

The other figure present motioned his head up and down to indicate the slow agreement of a man whose mind had worked along similar lines on countless occasions. This was Tim Dinsdale, an Englishman whose name is synonymous with the search for truth at Loch Ness. Fifteen years earlier, in 1960, he had taken a short cine film of one of the loch's strange inhabitants as it swam away across the surface. This film had rekindled world-wide interest in the mystery and led to a succession of largely futile attempts at solving it.

Largely futile, that is, until the summer of 1972, when Bob Rines and his American colleagues had produced the first piece of real evidence which shook the scientific establishment to its reactionary roots and forced it to start taking the Loch Ness mystery seriously. In August of that year one of his underwater cameras took a picture showing the flipper and side of a large animal at the same time as a sonar monitoring device recorded the passage of two thirty-foot-long moving objects. The photograph was developed under legal bond at the headquarters of the Eastman Kodak Company in America and was subsequently submitted for confidential study to, among others, the British Museum of Natural History and the American Smithsonian Institution.

Their public findings at that time constituted the first expressions of official scientific credence in a mystery which has now been in the public eye for nearly half a century and which has been the butt of so much ill-informed, whimsical comment that to most people it falls into the category either of the 'cunning tourist trap' or the 'product of a drunken Scotsman's imagination'. Such attitudes are entirely understandable: to those who have not studied the facts, the Loch Ness Monster is still merely one of those escapist fantasies so beloved by newspaper cartoonists and news editors in search of their 'silly season' stories.

However, the facts of the mystery, as related in full for the first time in this book, tell a very different story. They tell of the existence, in an overpopulated island in the civilized western world, of a species of unknown animal which may be the only living survivor from the age of the dinosaurs.

The key to the whole tortuous story is ignorance. Ignorance on the part of the general public is excusable; we rely on the media for the facts on which to base our understanding and judgement of any matter outside our direct experience. So when the facts that are presented are all trivialized and weighted against a proper understanding, let alone a judgement, it is not surprising that the reaction is one of profound suspicion. But ignorance among 'experts', who presume to make knowledgeable comments on a subject, is inexcusable.

Only recently I corresponded with one of Scotland's most eminent zoologists, who reviewed the first, hardback, edition of this book for a national newspaper. His review was critical of the whole subject. Fair enough. I wrote to him asking, as a matter of curiosity, his unofficial opinion of the 1972 Rines underwater results. He replied that he did not recall reading about them when he was preparing his review (in fact, they were highlighted in the opening paragraph of that edition and formed the climax to the book), and went on, rather curtly: 'This new "evidence" is all on a par with so much in the past [a puzzling verdict, since, by his own admission, he didn't know what the new evidence was] ... It is just a very good tourist attraction and satisfies the human need for "monsters".'

Such an observation is typical of many comments made since the 'Monster' first achieved international fame in 1933, when British and American papers were quick to dismiss the whole affair as a tourist gimmick. The world's media has generally adopted a similar line ever since. In 1968 the Soviet press published the following comment by one of their scientists: 'When it becomes necessary to distract readers from real problems, Western leaders have three sensational stories which never fail – Flying Saucers, the Loch Ness Monster and the Abominable Snowman'.

In Britain, the cautious scientific establishment has been less than receptive to any new evidence that has challenged the official view. The real importance of the Loch Ness story, as it will unfold in the following chapters, does not rest simply with the scientific significance of the creatures, tremendous though this is. One of the most fascinating aspects of this investigation is the way that twentieth-century science and society have reacted to an extraordinary phenomenon which has managed not just to slip through our neatly constructed intellectual and technological nets, but threatens to tear great holes in them.

As the old Highlander said that June evening above Urquhart Bay: 'Aye, they all think they're so smart down south, but we know the beasties are there, and that's all there is to it.'

Chapter Two

Background to a Mystery

From either end it stretches as far as the eye can see: a narrow trench of dark, inky water greater in length than the narrowest point of the English Channel. On either side rugged, sylvan mountains rise to heights of over 2,000 feet. This is Loch Ness, moody and secretive, the largest freshwater lake in Great Britain and the third deepest in Europe. A writer in 1808 observed: 'Travelling down the North side of Loch Ness a person of any taste must be struck with the sublimity of the scene. A sheet of water before him at one view, 22 miles long and apparently two miles broad, which is unquestionably the largest body of freshwater in Britain.'

The loch lies in the northernmost sector of the Great Glen, the scar-like fault running right across the North of Scotland from the Moray Firth to Loch Linnhe. Available evidence suggests that the Glen is a sinistral wrench fault, and that 300 to 400 million years ago, in a succession of tremors, the land cracked open and the area to the north of the fault slowly moved some sixty-five miles in a south-westerly direction.

The landform, lying like an open wound, was at the mercy of nature's erosive forces, and during the period of glacial action 25,000 to 10,000 years ago Loch Ness was gouged out by north-eastward-flowing glaciers of up to 4,000 feet in thickness. The whole of the Highland area was enveloped in ice, all, that is, except Britain's highest mountain, Ben Nevis, sixty miles south-west of Loch Ness, which has never been completely covered by ice.

Both before and after the period of glacial action Loch Ness is thought to have been an arm of the sea. The sedimentary deposits of Old Red Sandstone bordering much of the loch and the shell-bearing clay at Clava, five miles east of the town of Inverness, bear witness to this.

The glaciers created a narrow, steep-sided loch, 14,000 acres in surface area, twenty-four miles long, and up to one and a half miles wide. For much of its length Loch Ness is over 700 feet deep, and the maximum depth was once believed to be 754 feet. However, in 1969 a miniature submarine went down to a depth of 820 feet and recorded 975 feet on its depth-sounding apparatus. It is fair to say that the maximum depth of the loch is as yet unknown.

Judged by its estimated cubic capacity of 263,000 million cubic feet, Loch Ness is easily the largest freshwater body in the British Isles. Its volume contrasts with that of Loch Lomond, its superior in surface area but with a volume of only 93,000 million cubic feet; and Loch Morar, at 1,017 feet the deepest lake in Britain, which has a volume of only 81,000 million cubic feet. Compared to, say, America's Great Lakes Loch Ness is, of course, relatively small but it supports an abundant quantity of life.

Its waters are fresh and unpolluted and for the greater part of the year it is fished for salmon and trout; the record salmon for the loch is 52 lb., caught by a resident of Fort Augustus in the 1950s. In addition to these two migratory fish there are brown trout, an added attraction for the angler and perhaps also for any large predators in the loch. In the deeper water of the main loch are arctic char and an enormous quantity of eels, some of which are known to be quite large. No one has ever calculated the size of Ness' fish population, but since netting is prohibited there is no reason why it should not be very large.

The only major survey of the loch was carried out in the early years of this century. Its results, published in the Bathymetrical Survey of 1911, describe it as a long V-shaped rock-basin, the northern end of which is ponded by glacial and fluvio-glacial and raised beach deposits. The bottom was said to be 'as flat as a bowling green', although the subterranean sides are very steep. At Horseshoe Crag on the south-eastern side, a depth of 236 feet was recorded just 100 feet from the shore, and at Cormorant rock a similar depth was found only fifty feet from the shore, indicating an angle only 15° from the perpendicular.

Although the water is fresh it has a low pH factor, because of the suspension of peat particles brought down from the mountains by the numerous rivers and burns. At a depth of about fifty feet the water is opaque and, judging by divers' accounts, very frightening. Its acidity, combined with the steep sides, prevents any substantial plant growth in the water; it may also be the reason why an eighteenth-century writer recorded that the loch waters caused biliousness when drunk.

The temperature of the water is low. Research just after the turn of the century by Sir John Murray, and in 1953 by Dr C. H. Mortimer of the Freshwater Biological Association, indicated the presence of a surface warm layer about 150 feet in depth, the temperature of which varies according to the prevailing weather conditions. Below this layer, the loch contains colder, heavier water which remains at a fairly constant temperature of 42–44°F.

The climate is mild and damp. From 1921 to 1950 Fort Augustus, at the southern end of the loch, is recorded as having suffered the lowest annual hours of sunshine in Britain. Mist and squalls are channelled in from the sea along the length of the Great Glen, and the loch's placid surface can be whipped into a turmoil within minutes. Its catchment area is extensive, and during periods of heavy rain the loch surface can rise with alarming rapidity.

However, the loch itself never freezes, partly because of its great depth and volume of water; this acts as an enormous atmospheric heater during the winter months, preventing snow from lying in the immediate vicinity for any length of time. It has been calculated that the heat generated by the loch during winter is equivalent to that given off by the combustion of two million tons of coal.

So much for the basic geographical details of the setting. Imagine an area of mountain, forest and lake into which twentieth-century development has infiltrated slowly. This is the area where Britain's largest known animal, the red deer, is to be found; where her largest bird, the golden eagle, and her wildest

11

animal, the wild-cat, live, and where the wolf roamed until the last one was shot in Inverness in 1743.

It is set in a country which retains its proud independence from the rest of Britain; where the native language, Gaelic, is still spoken by many of the older generation and where the ancient tribal ties of the clan are still venerated. In such an area, where superstition has clearly manifested itself within modern times, one would expect there to be a legend concerning the source of the great lake.

Such a legend is recorded in William Mackay's book *Urquhart and Glenmoriston* (published privately in 1914); it is with the kind permission of his son that the following extract is included.

Legend says that the great glen which now lies under the waters of Loch Ness was a beautiful valley, sheltered from every blast by high mountains and clothed with trees and herbs of richest hues . . . There was a spring in this happy vale which was blessed by Daly the Druid and whose waters were ever afterwards an unfailing remedy for every disease. This holy well was protected by a stone placed over it by the Druid who enjoined that whenever the stone was removed for the drawing of water it should be immediately replaced. 'The day on which my command is disregarded,' said he, 'desolation will overtake the land.' The words of Daly were remembered by the people and became a law among them: and so day followed day and year gave place to year. But on one of the days a woman left the child of her bosom by the fireside and went to the well to draw water. No sooner did she remove the stone from its place than the cry reached her ear that the child had moved towards the fire. Rushing to the house, she saved the infant – but she forgot the word of the Druid and omitted to replace the stone. The waters rose and overflowed the vale, and the people escaped to the mountains and filled the air with lamentation, and the rocks echoed back the despairing cry – 'Tha loch 'nis ann, tha loch 'nis ann!' – 'There is a lake now, there is a lake now!' And the lake remained and it is called Loch Nis to this day.

The Highlands of Scotland were shrouded in the mists of obscurity until the beginning of the Middle Ages, when English troops first occupied the area. Legends abounded and one of these concerned the water horse or kelpie ('Each Uisge' in

Gaelic). Its favourite haunts were supposed to be lonely lochs, and the abundance of Highland lochs baptized 'na beiste' indicates the widespread belief in this mythical creature. It was said to be an evil spirit which lured weary travellers to their deaths, and it is undoubtedly this belief and subconscious association with the kelpie that are responsible for much of the historical reluctance of the Highlanders to talk about any real experiences with the creatures believed to be inhabiting Loch Ness.

Not until 1933 did the world hear about the Loch Ness 'Monster', and since then there have been regular reports of sightings every year. Before that date there were, by comparison, only a handful. The reason usually put forward for the lack of publicity before 1933 is that the area was remote and isolated and that the construction of an A-class road along the whole northern shore of the loch in 1933 was the spark which sent news of the animals spreading around the world.

This is largely true. And yet the Highlands were populated by many more people in past centuries than they are now. Furthermore, after the construction in the early nineteenth century of the Caledonian Canal, which itself brought hundreds of workers to the loch, the Great Glen became a fashionable area for the Victorian aristocracy, and paddle steamers plied up and down the loch daily. Yet there are comparatively few reports of a large animal being seen, certainly not sufficient for the loch to be associated with strange creatures in the minds of any but the local residents.

If a herd of large animals does exist in Loch Ness, one would expect visitors of past centuries, few in number though they may have been in comparison with the contemporary hordes, to have noticed and reported the fact. Before trying to explain this apparent paradox I shall describe, in chronological order, some of the pre-twentieth-century reports of Loch Ness animals that have come to light.

The first known record of a 'Monster' in the loch, as all students of the subject know so well, dates from 1,400 years ago, about A.D. 565. And the witness surely outstrips any of his modern counterparts in terms of standing, since he was a saint, no less.

St Columba, the man who brought the Christian religion to Scotland (there is a stone at the lochside village of Abriachan from which it is said he baptized the heathen Picts), was on his way to visit Brude, King of the Northern Picts in Inverness. His biographer, Adamnan, writes in his *Life of St Columba* (Volume 6, Book II, Chapter 27): 'Of the driving away of a certain water monster by the virtue of the prayer of the holy man'.

The Saint had arrived on the banks of Loch Ness at a place where there was a ferry coble. (It has been suggested that this was either at the mouth of the River Ness or near Urquhart.) There he found the Picts burying a man who had been bitten to death by a water monster while he was swimming. According to one version of the story, St Columba laid his staff upon the man's chest and brought him back to life. Another version relates that one of the Picts, rather than listen to the Saint's sermon, had swum off across the river or loch and was attacked and killed by the monster. When he heard of the man's death, St Columba ordered one of his men to swim across the water and return with the coble moored on the far side. Adamnan continues the story thus:

On hearing this direction of the holy and famous man, Lugne Mocumin, obeying without delay, throws off all his clothes except his tunic and casts himself into the water. But the monster, per-ceiving the surface of the water disturbed by the swimmer, suddenly comes up and moving towards the man rushed up with a great roar and open mouth. Then the blessed man, observing this, raised his holy hand ... invoking the name of God, formed the saving sign of the Cross in the air and commanded the ferocious monster saying, 'Thou shalt go no further nor touch the man; go back with all speed.' Then at the voice of the Saint the monster was terrified and fled more quickly than if it had been pulled back with ropes.

St Columba is also credited with another brush with the animals; there is a legend that the beast towed the Saint's boat across the loch and was granted its perpetual freedom.

One can only take these stories at their face value. However, if nothing else, it is a remarkable coincidence that Adamnan should record that St Columba encountered a 'water monster' in, of all the Scottish lochs, Loch Ness. Perhaps the story became exaggerated during its transmission to Adamnan, who wrote his biography a century after the event is said to have occurred. Perhaps it is an embellished version of a real incident involving a sighting of a large animal in the loch which was designed to demonstrate the power of Christian prayer. All we can do is note the stories as an auspicious start to the intriguing mystery.

The source of the next report of a 'Monster' in Loch Ness is a letter dated 17 October 1933 to *The Scotsman* newspaper from a Mr D. Murray Rose. He wrote:

The next reference to the monster of Loch Ness [i.e., after St Columba] appears in an old book dealing with curiosities – such as dragons, dog-devils, the dwarfs of Dalton. It mentions that the monster appeared in the year when Fraser of Glenvackie, after a 'sair tussle', killed a fire-spouting dragon . . . It goes on to say that Fraser killed the last known dragon in Scotland. But 'no one has yet managed to slay the monster of Loch Ness, lately seen'. We have independent reference to Fraser of Glenvackie's fight with the dragon, and the date is known to be about 1520. The 'beast' of Loch Ness was seen twice between 1600 and 1700. Patrick Rose of Rosehall, Demerera, who was born in the district, wrote some notes about his youthful adventures when fox hunting or after wild-cats in the country above Loch Ness. People told him that in the year when Sir Ewen Cameron of Lochiel had a fight with wild-cats on the shores of Loch Ness, a monster was seen in the loch . . . It appeared again in 1771 and people were convinced it was the 'water-kelpie'.

In the mid-seventeenth century, during the eleven years when Great Britain's monarchy was replaced by Oliver Cromwell's Commonwealth, a garrison of English soldiers was stationed in Inverness. Their task was to control the Highlands, and one of the steps taken to improve communications was to transport a ship from Inverness to Loch Ness on wooden rollers. The ship was launched on the loch in about 1655 and it was thereafter used to patrol it.

Amongst the men stationed in the Highlands was Richard Franck, a literary trooper in Cromwell's army. He wrote: 'The famous Lough Ness, so much discours'd for the supposed floating island; for here it is, if anywhere in Scotland.'

'The floating island.' Could this reference to unidentified floating objects on the surface of Loch Ness relate to the animals? Franck said that it was merely a mat of vegetation blown across the loch's surface. And yet vegetable mats do not exist on Loch Ness, because there is no vegetation in the water to form them. An interesting corollary to this appears in Blaeu's Atlas, which was published in 1653. It contains the following note against Loch Lomond: 'Waves without wind, fish without fin and a floating island.'

The eighteenth century was a period of great upheaval in Scottish history. The two Jacobite rebellions, in 1715 and 1745, and the subsequent victory of the English at the Battle of Culloden in 1746 led to widespread social and geographical changes throughout the Highlands. The Commander-in-Chief of the English army in Scotland, General Wade, was responsible for the construction of the first proper road along the loch side, from Fort Augustus up into the mountains behind the loch and back down through Foyers, Inverfarigaig and Dores and into Inverness. Work started in 1731, and several hundred soldiers were employed on a task which required considerable engineering skill. The miners who blasted away the terraces had to hang on the end of ropes so that they could bore into the rock and place the explosive charges.

In 1964, a correspondent in New Zealand claimed to have come across a book published in 1769 describing how 'Two Leviathan creatures were sighted upon several occasions in the loch by the road builders. It was thought these may have been one of the whale variety or some huge unknown sea species which had made their way through some subterranean passage and grown too large to return.' Attempts to trace the book from which the passage was taken have been unsuccessful, and so we are unfortunately left with unsubstantiated historical evidence of events which we can only say may have taken place.

Another claim which is similarly unsubstantiated so far has been made by an American writer, Mr John A. Keele. A few years ago he was browsing through the files of *The Atlantic Constitution*, a widely read newspaper on the eastern coast of the U.S.A., when, he claims, he came across a long feature article on the Loch Ness animals in a copy of the newspaper dated some time in the 1890s. At the time he paid little attention to it, since it was not the subject he was researching. Mr Keele writes: 'I did not read the piece in toto since it was a full page illustrated with a drawing very similar to the modern drawings ...' Attempts to trace the article have, again, so far been unsuccessful.

As we move nearer to the present day, greater reliance can be placed on the eye-witness accounts, since they are more specific in their details and less uncertain as to their sources. In 1802 Mr Alexander MacDonald, a crofter in the village of Abriachan, told one of the ancestors of Loch Ness' now retired water bailiff, Mr Alexander Campbell, that he had several times seen a strange animal in the loch. On one occasion he was rescuing a lamb that had fallen down the hill when one of the animals surfaced and swam to within fifty yards of him. He could see that it had short appendages with which it was propelling itself. Then it turned and proceeded out into the open loch until it submerged with a great commotion at a range of about 500 yards. Mr MacDonald said the animal appeared to be about twenty feet long and reminded him of a salamander. It is said that until he died he often referred to the animal as 'the great salamander'.

This is interesting because right into the early years of the present century, when the ferries used to put into Abriachan pier, the skipper would regularly hail the piermaster by shouting: 'Seen the salamander today, Sandy?'

Mr D. Mackenzie of Balnain wrote in 1934 to Commander Rupert T. Gould, author of *The Loch Ness Monster and Others* (Geoffrey Bles, 1934), the first book written on this subject: 'I saw it in about 1871 or 1872 as near as I can remember now – about 12 o'clock on a grand sunny day, so that it was impossible to be mistaken. It seemed to me to look rather like an upturned boat and went at great speed wriggling and churning up the water. I have told the same story to my friends long before the present Monster became famous.'

Then there is the dramatic story of a diver, Duncan MacDonald, who was sent to examine a sunken ship off the Fort

Augustus entrance to the Caledonian Canal in 1880. Soon after MacDonald was lowered into the water the men on the surface received frantic signals from him to be pulled up. When he did surface it is said his face was like chalk and he was trembling violently. It was several days before he would talk about the incident, but eventually he described how he had been examining the keel of the ship when he saw a large animal lying on the shelf of rock on which the wreck was lodged. 'It was a very odd-looking beastie,' he said, 'like a huge frog.' He refused to dive in the loch again.

In 1933 the late Duke of Portland wrote to *The Scotsman* (20 October) and *The Times* (10 November): 'I should like to say that when I became, in 1895, the tenant of the salmon angling in Loch Oich and the River Garry, the forester, the hotelkeeper and the fishing ghillies used often to talk about a horrible great beastie as they called it, which appeared in Loch Ness.'

In the summer of 1896 the animals are reported to have been seen on several occasions by the residents of Fort Augustus. Amongst the witnesses was Mr James Rose, a local shopkeeper, who saw a large hump-like object moving at speed along the loch.

And so the shreds of a historical record of strange animals in Loch Ness clearly exist, although the details are frequently clouded or temporarily lost through the passage of time. The local residents had neither any reason nor any desire to broadcast their superstitions and beliefs about the contents of the 'great water'. Often the borderline between superstition and objective belief was obscured. The local people all knew that the loch contained something – but what was it? Their ignorance about its true nature bred fear. Some, I have been told by an elderly resident, used to believe that the loch contained the devil itself and that the sight of one of its denizens was an evil omen.

Alex Campbell, the retired water bailiff who has himself had many sightings of the animals (as will be described later), was strictly instructed as a boy never to swim in the loch in case the kelpie took him. No wonder, therefore, that in such an atmosphere the local Highlanders displayed their traditional reticence and refrained from talking about what, to the small closely-knit communities, must have been a rather confidential subject and certainly not one to be bandied about amongst the frivolous nineteenth- and early-twentieth-century visitors brought to the area by the Caledonian Canal.

Information about the early sightings emerges only now, in a trickle of hard fact and hearsay conviction. Now that the subject has acquired a certain amount of fame and almost respectability, and Loch Ness has adjusted to its annual cosmopolitan atmosphere, the witnesses of older generations are more ready to place their experiences on record in the knowledge that they will at least have a receptive audience.

The *Inverness Courier* reported on 6 November 1962 on an outing of pensioners of the Caledonian Canal Authority. Conversation turned to the 'Monster', and under the heading 'Monster sightings recalled', the correspondent wrote:

As long ago as 1926, Mr Simon Cameron of Invergarry saw it for the first time near Cherry Island, at the Fort Augustus end of the loch. 'It was while I was watching two gulls skimming the loch's surface that my attention was fixed when the gulls suddenly rose screaming into the air,' he said. 'Then before my eyes, something like a large upturned boat rose from the depths and I can still see the water cascading down its sides. Just as suddenly, though, it sank out of sight, but it was an extraordinary experience.' Much older, however, is the experience that Mr Duncan Chisholm of Inverness told of. It goes back to the time of the Battle of Waterloo, when his mother's grand-aunt, Miss Bella MacGruer, at that time living at Markethill, Fort Augustus, warned the youth of the village not to go bathing in Loch Ness where she and others had frequently seen the 'water horse'.

The following two extracts from letters written to *The Scotsman* provide valuable additional information. The first takes us far back into the nineteenth century, and the second gives an insight into the stifling aura of superstition prevailing at the turn of the century. The first letter is dated 11 September 1950.

The late Dr Galbraith of Dingwall used to tell of how he was visiting on the west coast of this country, and while in a house there

19

a paper came in with an account of the Loch Ness Monster. With them in the house was a man who had returned home after spending most of his life in New Zealand. This New Zealander quietly said: 'I have seen the Loch Ness Monster.'

As a boy he had gone to help to take a boat from Plockton to Inverness. While they were sailing (there were no engines in those days) through Loch Ness with a steady wind behind them the Monster had suddenly 'heaved up alongside' and it continued on a parallel course for a very short distance.

I once met John MacGillivray from Invergarry at Inverness. I translate our talk about the Monster (we spoke in Gaelic) word for word.

'Did you come from Invergarry today?'

'I did.'

'Did you come by Loch Ness?'

'I did.'

'Did you see the Monster?'

'I did not. How old do you think I am?'

'You are about seventy years old, I imagine.'

'I am eighty-three years old,' he said, and drawing himself up, with a touch of assurance he added, 'and the Monster was in the loch before I was born and that was not yesterday.'

The second correspondent, who signed himself 'H. F. W.', wrote the following on 6 September 1957:

There is no doubt in my mind, and never was, that there was 'something odd' in Loch Ness, as the Fort Augustus Monastery people knew about it and I heard from them during the years of the South African War. It was common knowledge; but people did not like being laughed at and you only heard little bits as you got to know the people.

However, one night I got something to think about. I had been out on the hills after deer at Inchnacardoch with the keeper, and when we got to his house the three children were crying – a sort of hysterical crying. Husband and wife spoke Gaelic and I only had a fair smattering. He told his wife in no uncertain tones that he had warned her time and again that the children were not to go near Cherry Island in the gloaming. Later in the evening I tried to 'draw' him about it, but beyond saying that no one ever knew what might be in a loch like that, I was left guessing ... but it was clear that they knew or thought something was in the loch. The odd thing was that no one ever thought of not going fishing in the loch for salmon; and it might have been that they did not wish the visitors to know. I subsequently, after the first war, had a talk with a priest with whom I had been friends for years, and he frankly said that the story had been going around to his knowledge since before the monastery was built.

*

From these accounts it would appear that the belief in the existence of unknown animals in Loch Ness is as old as the Christian religion in the Highlands of Scotland. The animals have existed in obscurity, roaming the black depths of the loch, occasionally showing themselves and adding a new strand to be woven into the fabric of Highland legend. It is understandable that many of the eye-witness stories have been lost, since the subject was suppressed by the local people for fear of its unpleasant consequences and associations.

The opening up of the Highlands and, in particular, of the Great Glen was a gradual process from the beginning of the nineteenth century. Until just two hundred years ago visitors ventured into the Highlands at their peril. The construction of General Wade's military road has already been mentioned. On the other bank, the northern, which now carries the A82 major route, a track ran along the hilltops from Inverness to Castle Urquhart and from there across the flank of Mealfuarvonie and into Glenmoriston. This was the route taken by the English and Scottish soldiers of Edward I in the thirteenth century as they fought for control of the Highlands.

Credit for the first step in opening the Great Glen as an attraction to visitors is undoubtedly due to Thomas Telford, the designer and engineer of the Caledonian Canal. The Canal links the three freshwater lochs in the Great Glen (Ness, Oich and Lochy) to form a sixty-mile-long waterway joining the North Sea to the Atlantic Ocean. It took nineteen years to build and was opened in 1822. Its construction raised the level of Loch Ness by about six feet.

Several hundred men were employed on building the Canal and in 1818 over 200 of them were working in Fort Augustus. With so much activity near the loch one would expect there to be some mention of the animals; and in a letter to *The Scotsman* dated 10 September 1957 a Mrs Joan Grieve wrote: 'I would like to say that my grandfather was for some time employed by the company which built the Caledonian Canal. He repeatedly referred to a strange creature living in Loch Ness, having seen it himself. He lived to be a centenarian and died over 60 years ago.' It is not clear whether the writer's grandfather saw the creatures while he was working on the Canal. One can presume that since many of the Canal workers were local men they must have been aware of the stories.

The journey through the lochs on one of the paddle steamers became a fashionable leisure activity for rich visitors to the Highlands. In 1873 Queen Victoria travelled down the Canal and remarked: 'The Caledonian Canal is a very wonderful piece of engineering but travelling on it is very tedious.' In the same year a certain Gordon Cumming, a well-known big-game hunter, regularly made the trip through the Canal accompanied by his servant and long-bearded goat. He was himself quite an attraction – on hot days he often paraded without his kilt. Presumably he was unaware of the greatest of all potential quarries beneath his very feet as the steamers pounded their way along Loch Ness.

*

The summer at Loch Ness today is a flurry of visitor activity. Cars, coaches and caravans ring the loch with steel and glass; motor cruisers and yachts vie for space on the water. Five miles north-east of the loch is the town of Inverness with 35,000 inhabitants, the 'Capital of the Highlands' which each year copes with the tourist invasion with increasing difficulty. From Inverness the traveller to Loch Ness has a choice of either the modern highway, the A82, or a greatly improved version of General Wade's old road. Each leads to one side of the loch and they eventually join again at Fort Augustus at its southern tip.

Between Inverness and Fort Augustus the A82 clings to the loch's side apart from two detours at the villages of Drumnadrochit and Invermoriston. For most of the distance the traveller's view of the water from the road is obscured by bushes and trees which exasperate the many pairs of watchful eyes peering anxiously from speeding cars.

Drumnadrochit was a popular resting place for nineteenth-century travellers, and lines in the old visitors' books of the village inn attest to the popularity of the place. In 1860, Shirley Brooks wrote in a letter to *Punch* magazine: 'If there were many places like Drumnadrochit persons would be in fearful danger of forgetting that they ought to be miserable.'

South of Drumnadrochit and its neighbour Lewiston, the road returns to the lochside and runs on – past Strone, 'the nose', where the ancient ruins of Castle Urquhart are perched below the road – past the stone memorial to John Cobb, who died on Loch Ness in 1952 whilst attempting to break the world water speed record in his boat *Crusader* – past Achnahannet, until 1972 the headquarters of the Loch Ness Investigation Bureau, and on through Forestry Commission pine forests and under the eaves of Mealfuarvonie.

At Invermoriston the road makes another loop through the village. A few miles up Glenmoriston, away from Loch Ness, is Dundreggan, which means the 'Hill of the Dragon'. Here too are 'The Footprints'. These are said to date from 1827 when a travelling preacher tried to conduct a sermon at the spot. A couple of young men started to heckle and throw things at him, at which the preacher is said to have retorted that the ground on which he stood would bear witness to the truth of what he said until the Day of Judgement. Marks in the solid rock, visible today, are said to be his footprints.

It was across these mountains and moors that Bonnie Prince Charlie made his escape after the defeat at Culloden. For a time he lived in a cave near Glenmoriston, protected by the celebrated 'Seven Men of Glenmoriston', who carried on a private guerrilla war against the English Redcoats swarming over the mountains in search of the Prince.

These were desperate times for the Highland people. William Augustus, the Duke of Cumberland, youngest son of King George II, after whom Fort Augustus was named in 1742 (its old name was Kilcumein, meaning the Church of Cumein, one of St Columba's successors), moved his entire army to Fort

Augustus and ordered his men to spread out through the glens and show no mercy in suppressing the native population. Houses were destroyed and people murdered in their hundreds. Cattle and sheep were herded together and driven back to Fort Augustus to be sold to dealers from the south. The local people took refuge in the mountains, where many died of hunger and disease. Others left their homes for good and emigrated to America and the other colonies. Those that remained found themselves deprived of their land as clan chiefs rented vast stretches to southern sheep farmers. They were even prevented from wearing their traditional dress, the plaid; an Act of Parliament prohibited it in 1746.

Fort Augustus, the scene of so much brutality and bloodshed two hundred years ago, is now the largest settlement on the shores of Loch Ness. The fort from which the town's new name derived was completed in 1742 by General Wade and played a significant part in the troubles described above. However, the fort is now gone and, ironically, in its place now stands a monastery. The fort was sold in 1876 for £5,000 to Lord Lovat, whose son bequeathed it to the English congregation of Benedictine monks who converted the site.

Northwards from Fort Augustus, General Wade's old route makes a precipitous climb up the mountains to the east of the loch, from the top of which one gains an imposing panoramic view of the town and of the loch stretching into the far distance, before the road plunges away from the lochside across an area of barren Highland landscape. For fourteen miles the route meanders across moorland, dodges tiny lochs and scales hills before dropping down a narrow, perilously winding track to Foyers and the loch again.

The village of Foyers is famous for two things. First the aluminium works, started in 1896 and which at one time produced the greatest quantity of aluminium in the world. The smelting was made possible by the use of hydro-electric power (the first in Great Britain), which in turn was made possible by the River Foyers and the village's second claim to fame, the Falls of Foyers.

The river makes two falls during its thirteen-mile run across the mountains, one of forty feet and the other of ninety feet. The spray rising from the latter has given it the name of 'Eas na-smud' – 'The Fall of Smoke' – and inspired the great Scottish poet Robert Burns to write:

> Among the heathy hills and rugged woods
> The foaming Foyers pours his mossy floods,
> Till full he dashes on the rocky mounds
> Where through a shapeless breach his stream resounds.
> As high in air the bursting torrents flow
> As deep recoiling surges down below.
> Prone down the rock the whitening sheet descends
> And viewless Echo's ear, astonished rends.
> Dim seen through rising mist and ceaseless showers
> The hoary cavern wide resounding low'rs
> Still through the gap the struggling river toils
> And still below the horrid cauldron boils.

The aluminium works closed in 1967, and since then extensive work has been done on a £10-million hydro-electricity scheme designed to provide power for Inverness. The scheme involves driving a tunnel through the rock from Foyers to Loch Mhor, nearly 600 feet up in the mountains, and sinking the power station into the ground below the surface of Loch Ness. About 500 men have been employed on the work over the past four years and many sightings of the animals have been reported by them.

One mile north of Foyers lies the hamlet of Boleskine, recognizable by the tiny graveyard below the road and Boleskine House immediately above it. From 1900 to 1918 this was the home of the infamous Aleister Crowley, the self-styled 'Great Beast' of black magic, and 'the wickedest man in the world', according to the press. It is said that Crowley terrorized the local people and drove several of his servants mad. Nowhere in his writings is there any reference to unknown animals in Loch Ness.

Whilst at Boleskine, Crowley demonstrated his peculiarly warped sense of humour by writing to the Secretary of the Vigilance Society that 'I am sorry to say that prostitution in this neighbourhood is most unpleasantly conspicuous.' At which the

Society sent a special observer to Foyers to investigate. Not surprisingly, he found nothing and when Crowley was informed of this he wrote back: 'Conspicuous by its absence, you fools!' The house is now in the hands of a member of one of the world's most popular rock groups.

Another mile further north is the village of Inverfarigaig, a tiny cluster of houses and cottages nestling in a clearing above the loch. Running east from the village is Inverfarigaig Pass, a narrow cleft in the mountains, on one side of which is a granite outcrop known as Black Rock. The summit of this crag bears the remains of a 2,000-year-old vitrified fort called Dun Deardail. This is said to have been the residence of an Irish folk hero called Nysus who was the first person ever to set out by boat and explore Loch Ness, thereby ensuring that the loch would bear a modified version of his own name.

Continuing on our imaginary tour we pass special clearances on the loch side of the road where brief uninterrupted views of the water can be enjoyed. Elsewhere the undergrowth is thick and the terrain largely inhospitable both below and above the road. Finally we come to the village of Dores, situated on the north-eastern corner of the loch, from where the shore leads around to a shallow, sandy beach consisting of the deposits left by the ancient glaciers. Here the whole vista of Loch Ness spreads out before one. The dome-shaped cap of Meal-fuarvonie protrudes from the mountain line on the right, and in the distance the water rises to meet the sky. On a calm day the surface resembles a sheet of darkly stained glass, reflecting the mountains and sky and giving a deceptively innocent impression of its hidden, abyssal depths.

*

This then is the scene of our mystery: an enormous volume of water situated in a corner of Britain which retains much of the atmosphere of wild remoteness of former ages despite the regular flow of traffic along the arteries on its banks and the yearly influx of visitors.

We have travelled rapidly from the distant past right into our own century and found a history of unknown creatures in Loch

Ness throughout. Next we turn to the near past and the events which transformed the intermittent trickle of 'Monster' stories into a raging torrent that overflowed the confines of the Loch Ness district and grabbed the world's attention in the winter of 1933–1934.

In 1773, Dr Samuel Johnson rode along Loch Ness and wrote: 'Natural philosophy is now one of the favourite studies of the Scottish nation and Loch Ness well deserves to be diligently studied.'

Loch Ness has surely lived up to the doctor's hopes.

Chapter Three

The 'Monster' Is Born

The 1930s dawned in an atmosphere of grave international economic depression. In Britain millions were unemployed; in the United States the figure was even more disturbingly large. This was the world in which two 'monsters' made their newspaper-headline debuts in 1933. At Loch Ness one began as a seven-week wonder and provided the world with a certain amount of light entertainment. The other, in Germany, started the preparations which were eventually to dominate the headlines and lead the world to the brink of self-destruction.

Along the northern shore of Loch Ness the new road was being completed. Vast amounts of rock had been blasted out of the mountainsides and pitched into the water below. Extensive areas of forest and scrubland had been cleared away to allow the road's passage, and unhampered views of the loch surface could now be obtained with ease and in comfort.

It was along this new road on the spring afternoon of 14 April 1933 that Mr and Mrs John Mackay set out for a peaceful drive from Inverness back to their home in Drumnadrochit. As they approached Abriachan Mrs Mackay, who was gazing out across the loch's serene surface, suddenly cried in surprise to her husband: 'Look, John, what's that – out there?'

She pointed to where, in the centre of the loch, the tranquillity had been replaced by a surging mass of water. Mr Mackay jammed on his brakes and for several minutes both of them watched 'an enormous animal rolling and plunging' until it disappeared with a great upsurge of water.

Mr and Mrs Mackay were the owners of the Drumnadrochit

Hotel, which fact will no doubt provoke wry grins among a good many sceptics. However, they never sought publicity for their story and nothing more would have been heard of it if it had not come to the attention of Alex Campbell, then a young water bailiff in Fort Augustus and the local correspondent for the *Inverness Courier*. He knew Mr and Mrs Mackay personally and therefore had no hesitation in writing the story up and delivering the copy to the *Courier*'s then editor, Dr Evan Barron.

The tale goes that when Dr Barron saw Alex Campbell's report he said 'Well, if it is as big as Campbell says it is we can't just call it a creature; it must be a real monster.' Thus the animals were christened with a title that has stuck ever since. The report of the sighting finally appeared as one of the *Courier*'s leading stories in its issue of 2 May 1933, and this is traditionally credited with being the start of the long saga of the 'Monster'.

However, this was not the first occasion on which the local press had reported the sighting of an unidentified animal in Loch Ness. On 27 August 1930 the *Northern Chronicle* had reported how 'Three young men from Inverness, the sons of well-known businessmen, had a curious experience the other evening on Loch Ness.' One of the young men was Mr Ian Milne, now the manager of a gunsmith's shop in Inverness. He described to me what happened:

It was at about 7 p.m. on 22 July 1930 when three of us were in a boat fishing off Tor Point near Dores. The loch was very calm, too calm for fishing to be worthwhile in fact, and I was amusing myself trying to see how far I could cast when I heard and saw a commotion about 600 yards up the loch. I saw spray being thrown up into the air to a considerable height ... it continued until it was about 300 yards away and then whatever was causing it turned southwards in a large half circle and moved away from us. It must have been travelling at about fifteen knots. My estimation of the length of the part of it we saw would be about twenty feet, and it was standing three feet or so out of the water. The wash it created caused our boat to rock violently ... It was without doubt a living

29

creature and since I spend a good deal of time in contact with wildlife I can say that it was certainly not a basking shark or a seal or a school of otters or anything normal.

Under its account of this sighting the *Northern Chronicle* published an appeal for further information on the phenomenon. A week later, on 3 September 1930, it printed several letters from people who described their own or other people's experiences on the loch. One correspondent, an 'Invernessian', wrote that about forty years earlier the skipper and crew of a canal steamer had seen a monster animal or fish while on passage through the loch.

Loch Ness was in the national news in 1932, though not because of any association with unidentified animals, of which there was no mention. On Sunday 28 August of that year Mrs Olaf Hambro, wife of a famous London banker, drowned in the loch whilst trying to swim to safety after an explosion on the boat on which she was travelling. The tragedy occurred off Glendoe boathouse, just south of the remote Horseshoe area of the loch's coastline.

A couple of days later three professional divers were hired to try to recover the body, and it was the activities of these divers which were largely responsible for the alarming stories of vast underwater caverns and treacherous currents. It is said that the divers were hauled to the surface in a state of gibbering shock, with their hair suddenly turned white and full of stories about caves like the interiors of great cathedrals. The truth is that the divers went down to about 150 feet, where they found they could see nothing because of the loch's impenetrable gloom. They returned to the surface, shaken and no doubt determined to avoid excessive work in such an eerie atmosphere.

*

Tracing the development of the 'Monster' story in the summer, autumn and winter of 1933 provides an interesting example of the media at work. Here was an immediately attractive story coming at a time when the press badly needed relief from the otherwise gloomy news. At first the approach was serious, but this soon gave way to flippant, idle 'bashing'.

Since 1933 several newspapers have vied with each other for the credit of having discovered 'Nessie'* in the summer of 1933. Although the *Inverness Courier*'s report of the Mackay sighting can claim to have been the original catalyst, the publicity was nevertheless slow in gathering momentum. By June the Scottish *Daily Express*, then operating from Glasgow, was carrying regular but rather cautious reports of events at the loch. The following are extracts from some of them.

9 June 1933:

Mystery fish in Scottish loch – Monster reported at Fort Augustus. A monster fish which for years has been somewhat of a mystery in Loch Ness was reported to have been seen yesterday at Fort Augustus.

28 June 1933:

Two men and two women who were boating on Loch Ness had an unpleasant and exciting experience today. The 'monster' rose out of the water about 50 yards from where the boat was drifting. One of the women fainted.

12 August 1933:

An effort to photograph the Loch Ness Monster is to be made by Captain Ellisford, a well known amateur photographer. He arrived in Inverness today with a large box of modern photographic material. He will use a telephoto lens.

Evidence that the mystery had not really caught the public eye by the end of the long and very hot summer of 1933 (it was the hottest on record) is afforded by the absence of any reference to the 'Monster' in a report, published on 13 September, by the local Tourist Board stating that the season had been a record one for visitors to the loch.

The excitement really began in October. By this time one of the animals had been seen crossing a lochside road (see Chapter 6), and over twenty accounts of water sightings had been reported since the Mackay sighting. One such occurred at about

* 'Nessie' is the affectionate nickname bestowed upon the animals by the press in 1933. By the end of the year they were also, for some completely unknown reason, being referred to as 'Bobby'.

11 a.m. on the morning of 22 September 1933, when the Reverend W. E. Hobbes of Wroxeter arrived at the Half-Way teahouse near Altsaigh (now a Youth Hostel) with his wife and sister-in-law. They walked in and found the room deserted. They called out and a voice from upstairs replied: 'We can't come down yet – we are looking at the Monster.'

The three visitors hurried up the stairs and found three other people, Miss Janet Fraser, Mrs G. Fraser and Miss M. Howden, standing on a balcony watching an object moving in the loch about half a mile away. At the front was a snake-like head and neck which was moving up and down and turning from side to side. Miss Fraser remarked that the head, in profile, was hardly wider than the neck. She thought she could see a large, glittering eye on its near side. The rest of the party all saw two low humps sitting in the water and a tail of indefinite length which splashed on the surface. The animal – for none of the witnesses was in any doubt that they were watching a living object – remained in view for about ten minutes before moving slowly away and sinking.

Distance deterred any attempts at estimating size but for it to be visible at that range its proportions must have been quite considerable. Mr Hobbes wrote: 'My wife and her sister were naturally excited at beholding this marvellous sight, but the proprietress of the teashop (Miss Fraser) took the matter quite calmly, remarking that she had seen the "Monster" three times before.'

In the second week of October 1933 *The Scotsman* became the first newspaper to send its own correspondent to the loch. The journalist assigned was Mr P. A. Stalker, who was with the Home Fleet at Invergordon when he received a message from the paper's chief reporter, Mr J. W. Herries, to go to Loch Ness and carry out his own investigation. Stalker recalls that the news caused 'more merriment than serious interest' in the wardroom of the destroyer at the time (*The Scotsman*, 16 June 1956). Nevertheless, he journeyed to Loch Ness and there spoke to a number of the people who claimed to have seen one of the animals. 'It didn't take me long to decide that, with one or two probable exceptions, the witnesses were telling the truth,' he reported.

The first of his three long articles appeared in *The Scotsman* on 16 October, a date which could be considered as Nessie's 'Glorious Twelfth'. London newspapers immediately sent teams of correspondents galloping north. By 18 October the *Daily Mail* and the *Daily Express* had begun their own inquiries, and on 23 October both carried special reports. The *Daily Express* gave theirs the whole of the back page, under the chilling headline 'Loch Ness Monster Hunted in Its Watery Lair'. Percy Cater, the *Daily Mail*'s man-on-the-spot, wrote breathlessly:

In Inverness, the Highland Capital, there is one topic of conversation – 'the beast' as by one accord everybody dubs the uncanny denizen of the loch by this sinister title. Some think the loch harbours a survivor of some prehistoric creature which may have been released from the earth's recesses by the great blasting operations required for the making of the new Inverness–Glasgow motor road.

Radio programmes were interrupted to accommodate the latest news from the loch. Letters began to pour into the offices of the Fishery Board for Scotland suggesting methods of capturing the creature. The Traffic Commissioners granted special permission for an express coach service to be run between Glasgow and Inverness to convey the inquisitive to the lochside. The Caledonian Canal, which had been losing a lot of traffic in recent years, suddenly found itself swamped by people wanting to tour the loch by boat. A special passenger steamer, *Princess Louise*, was laid on to travel between Inverness and Fort Augustus and was an immediate success.

Pleasing as this undoubtedly must have been to the local traders, the loch's sudden popularity was not to everybody's liking. In particular the local kirk complained about 'monster-hunters' breaking the Sabbath. The Rev. Murdo Campbell of Fort Augustus's Free Church complained indignantly:

One of the most pathetic sights which came under the observation of sane people in these parts within recent months was the presence of a number of people who arrived from the South last Lord's Day with a view to seeing a harmless animal which is supposed to reside

33

in the depths of Loch Ness. It now appears that a wise Providence prevented the animal from gratifying the eyes of these breakers of the Lord's Day. This leads me to say that the word 'monster' is really not applicable to the Loch Ness animal but it is truly applicable to those who deliberately sin against the light of law and revelation. [Scottish *Daily Express*, 2 November 1933]

Undaunted, the monster-hunters persisted in their investigations. Parties of boy scouts and ramblers and other diverse collections broke out their box cameras, lit their lochside camp fires, set up their deck-chairs and waited hopefully.

Looking back to the press reports of the almost carnival-like atmosphere of forty years ago it is hard not to be touched by the earnest and somewhat innocent optimism displayed by the searchers. For instance, there is a report of a group of forty Glasgow ramblers who spent six hours tramping through rain and mist. 'They then gave up the search, but three of them are to remain at Loch Ness for the next two or three days to see if they can trace any sign of the Monster.'

His Majesty's Government became involved when Sir Murdoch Macdonald, M.P. for Inverness-shire, wrote to the Secretary of State for Scotland, Sir Godfrey Collins, on 13 November:

As I have no doubt you are aware, some animal or fish of an unusual kind has found its way into Loch Ness. I think I can say the evidence of its presence can be taken as undoubted. Far too many people have seen something abnormal to question its existence. So far, there has been no indication of its being a harmful animal or fish and until somebody states the genus to which it belongs, I do hope you can authorise the police in the district to prevent pot-hunters deliberately looking for it. I have indeed been asked to bring a Bill into Parliament for its protection. I do not suggest this now because nobody yet knows what the animal or fish really is.

Sir Godfrey replied two days later:

I have been in communication with the Chief Constable of Inverness-shire who has informed me that five constables are stationed at different places on the loch, but that none of them has seen the Monster. The Chief Constable has, however, offered to cause warning to be given to as many of the residents and visitors as possible, for the purpose of preventing any attempt on the animal, if sighted, and I have told him that I shall be glad if he will do so.

This attempt to protect the animals seemed to be justified when Bertram Mills' Circus announced the offer of a £20,000 reward for the live capture of the 'Monster'. They apparently considered that there was a real risk of having to pay the reward, since they took out an insurance policy with Lloyds of London which cost them £80. Their offer was soon followed up by one of £5,000 from the New York Zoological Park and a private offer of £1,000.

However, 'Nessie' was not being taken seriously by everybody. Amongst those enjoying quiet chuckles or disparaging snorts at the time was one of the roadmen on the new motor road, and virtually the entire scientific community.

The roadman apparently used to evoke incredulous gasps from visitors by telling them that one night the 'Monster' came ashore and ate ten bags of cement stored in a council shed. Such a remark immediately strikes one as being quite absurd. However, when it is compared with the public pronouncements of a number of scientific experts it does not appear to be so comparatively lacking in wisdom.

For instance Professor D. M. Watson of University College, London, suggested that the 'Monster' was: 'a large lump of waterlogged peat floating round Loch Ness at the mercy of wind and currents'. Mr P. C. Grimshaw of the Royal Scottish Museum wrote: 'In our opinion the creature will probably turn out to be a young beluga or white whale.' A Professor Ritchie wrote to say that since the Stronsay Sea Serpent of a hundred years ago had turned out to be a decomposed shark, the Loch Ness Monster obviously could not be what it was claimed to be.

Perhaps the classic example of the pawky impotence of the establishment's sense of inquiry came from the Director of the Aquarium at the London Zoo, Mr E. G. Boulenger. He wrote:

The case of the Monster in Loch Ness is worthy of our consideration if only because it presents a striking example of mass hallucination. For countless centuries a wealth of weird and eerie

legend has centred round this great inland waterway . . . Any person
with the slightest knowledge of human susceptibility should therefore
find no difficulty in understanding how the animal, once being said
to have been seen by a few persons, should have shortly after revealed itself to many more . . . [*Observer*, 29 October 1933]

There is, one must admit, an element of truth in what Mr
Boulenger wrote. Auto-suggestion, the preconceived idea
brought to life by the desire to see something, does indeed play
its part in Loch Ness sightings. However, it is more than disturbing that none of those who criticized well-meaning witnesses ever visited the loch to examine either them or the
environment at first hand.

One man who did visit the loch was Commander Rupert T.
Gould, a prominent member of the BBC's *Brains Trust* radio
programme, a man whose insatiable curiosity had made him an
authority on subjects as diverse as the identity of the Man in the
Iron Mask and Arctic exploration. He arrived at Loch Ness in
November and began the research which eventually led him to
write *The Loch Ness Monster and Others* (1934), a careful
documentation of all the evidence available at that time.

In the absence of a specimen to parade triumphantly under
the raised eyebrows of the sceptics, all efforts at the loch were
being directed towards obtaining photographic evidence of the
animals' existence. It is a humbling thought that the search is
still going on, although now reaching its final, successful
phase.

The first known photograph said to be of one of the animals
was taken on 13 November 1933 by Mr Hugh Gray, an em-
ployee of the British Aluminium Company at Foyers. Mr Gray
was later interviewed by Bailie Hugh MacKenzie, J.P., in Inverness, when he swore the following statement:

Four Sundays ago after church, I went for my usual walk near
where the Foyers river enters the loch. The loch was like a mill
pond and the sun shining brightly. An object of considerable dimensions rose out of the water not so very far from where I was. I
immediately got my camera ready and snapped the object which was
then two to three feet above the surface of the water. I did not see
any head, for what I took to be the front parts were under the

water, but there was considerable movement from what seemed to be the tail, the part furthest from me. The object only appeared for a few minutes then sank out of sight.

Mr Gray had seen and photographed the object from a distance of an estimated 200 yards and from a height of thirty to forty feet above the water. He declined to estimate its size, except that it was 'very great'. The surface of it appeared to be smooth and glistening and to be a dark grey colour. It created a considerable disturbance in the water, which obscured a clear view of it.

Mr Gray took five shots of the object and then went home, where he put the camera and film away. It wasn't until a fortnight later that his brother removed the film and took it to an Inverness chemist for processing. Mr Gray explained his reluctance to take the film in himself: 'From the brief view I had of the object so far as the photo was concerned I thought nothing would show ... I might have had it developed long before I did but I was afraid of the chaff which the workmen and others would shower upon me.'

The photograph appeared in the *Daily Record* and *Daily Sketch* on 6 December, accompanied by statements by staff of the Kodak Company that the negative was untouched. Reaction from the scientific community was predictable. As F. W. Holiday wrote in his book *The Great Orm of Loch Ness* (page 29): 'Like a street musician, zoologists seemed limited to the one tune, and given a heaven sent chance to play at the Carnegie Hall, their limitations became plain.'

Mr J. R. Norman of the British Museum of Natural History remarked: 'I am afraid that the photo does not bring the mystery any nearer to a solution. It does not appear to me to be the picture of any living thing. My personal opinion is that it shows a rotting tree-trunk which rises to the loch surface when gas has generated in its cells.' One wonders where our 'experts' would be without the ubiquitous rotting tree-trunk and the decaying mat of vegetation.

With the publication of Hugh Gray's photograph, monster-fever swelled to unprecedented proportions. For the next six weeks not a day passed without some fresh news about the subject in the press. The first film which was claimed to show one of the animals was taken on 12 December by Mr Malcolm Irvine of Scottish Film Productions. He had deployed a small team of cameramen around the loch for two weeks before taking the film himself from the hillside opposite Urquhart Castle. He described what happened: 'We were so excited and elated when the Monster appeared that we had no time to think of the still cameras. What you actually see of the Monster on the screen lasts less than a minute, but it seemed hours when we were taking it. It definitely is something with two humps – that much is clear from the picture.'

The film was shot at a range of about one hundred yards with a cine camera fitted with a three-inch lens. The object, according to Mr Irvine, 'sailed along the surface at nine to ten m.p.h., leaving a trail of foam. We could see two portions of its back.'

By now there were scores of newsmen at the loch from all over the world, falling over each other in desperate attempts to find an exclusive scrap of information. In a review of the events of 1933, the French press decided that the year's only bright spot was the 'discovery' of the 'Monster'. The Austrian Government expressed indignation and claimed it was all an ingenious Scottish trick to keep tourists away from Austria. The British Prime Minister, Ramsay MacDonald, was reported to have been so keenly interested in the phenomenon that he planned a special trip to the loch in the hope of catching a glimpse. At Loch Ness fishermen complained that salmon had been scarcer than normal; 'Nessie' was naturally blamed.

On the same day that Malcolm Irvine was filming a moving object in the loch, the animals were the topic of a short debate in Parliament. Sir Murdoch Macdonald and Mr William Anstruther-Gray asked the Government what steps they proposed to take to investigate and resolve the matter. Sir Murdoch proposed trawls of the loch; Mr Anstruther-Gray favoured Air Force patrols.

Their suggestions caused temporary amusement and no more. The Government had more pressing problems, and Sir Godfrey Collins declared that he felt the search was a matter for private individuals and for the private enterprise of scientists, 'aided by the zeal of the press and photographers'. As an indication of the scale of interest in the subject at the time, this debate was reported widely throughout the world – including mention in such distant newspapers as the *Madras Mail* and the *Palestine Post*.

One British newspaper in particular determined to rise to the occasion. The *Daily Mail* announced that it was to engage a famous big-game hunter to track 'Nessie' down. Sadly, and through no fault of the sponsors, it was perhaps this expedition more than anything which was to destroy whatever credibility the animals had established.

Mr M. A. Wetherall, a Fellow of the Royal Geographical Society and the Royal Zoological Society, arrived in Inverness with his photographer, Mr Gustave Pauli, and a *Daily Mail* journalist, Mr F. W. Memory, in mid-December. They hired a boat and within a few days of their arrival they stumbled across strange footprints on the loch shore near Dores.

The 21 December edition of the *Mail* carried a large headline: 'Monster of Loch Ness is not a Legend but a Fact'. Mr Wetherall was quoted as saying:

It is a four-fingered beast and it has feet or pads about eight inches across. I should judge it to be a very powerful soft-footed animal about 20 feet long. The spoor I have found clearly shows the undulations of the pads and the outlines of the claws and nails ... I am convinced it can breathe like a hippopotamus or crocodile with just one nostril out of the water.

The spoor I found is only a few hours old, clearly demonstrating that the animal is in the neighbourhood where I expected to find it.

Mr Wetherall was unwise enough to say that he pledged his reputation that the spoor was genuine. On 23 December he broadcast his findings on the BBC. His talk was introduced as being 'something to freeze your blood' and was preceded (appropriately, as it turned out) by a comic newsreel.

Just as thirty-nine years later the BBC television newsroom was to show discretion over the apparent discovery of a dead 'monster' at Loch Ness on the afternoon before April Fool's

Day, whilst the rival channel made it the headline story on its 6 p.m. news bulletin, so in 1933 the rest of Fleet Street seemed to sense something amiss about Mr Wetherall's hoof-prints.

Not even *The Times* could resist taking a poke at the affair, and on 22 December it published the following amusing parody:

Owing largely to the encouragement of 'The Times' an expedition has set out at once for Loch Ness under the experienced leadership of Admiral Sir Chauncery Foulenough, the big-game hunter. The expedition will include speedboats, divers, film companies, geologists, archaeologists, zoologists, palaeontologists, seaplanes, gillies, expert shots, fishermen, whale hunters, cheese fanciers, bootboys and Stinkerbelle, the well known fairy. The aim of the expedition is to drain the loch, send down divers and then shoot Wendy from seaplanes. Two geologists were bitten yesterday, one by a diplodocus, and the other by Seacale, the Admiral's borzoi.

The London *Evening Standard* began to publish the daily adventures of their imaginary couple, Messrs Low and Terry, aboard their trawler *The Finnan Haddock*. 'As you see, we have fastened an iron ring to the stern of the boat. This we shall put through the creature's nose,' exclaimed Mr Low in one of the first instalments.

Even F. W. Memory, the *Mail*'s man, appeared to have misgivings about the find and recorded a conversation with Mr Wetherall in which he pointed out that he had been phenomenally lucky to discover the spoor in only four days. The big-game hunter replied that it was not luck but the triumph of experience, gained after tracking big-game over thousands of miles. It is perhaps cruel to point out that Mr Wetherall apparently failed to notice that both the prints had been made with the same foot – a right hind one.

Plaster casts were made with appropriate solemnity and publicity and dispatched to the British Museum of Natural History for examination. (*The Times* reacted to this by reporting that its expedition had taken a plaster cast of a large ear-mark found on a fern by the roadside!) However, the world had to wait in suspense over the Christmas holiday, and many people tried to satisfy their curiosity by journeying to Loch Ness. The press reported that 'monster-hunting parties' suddenly became ultra-fashionable and filled all the local hotels. Inverness was floodlit for the first time in its history, and rail travellers were welcomed at the station by a special display of fairy-lights. It was reported that on Boxing Day cars formed an almost continuous line from Inverness down to Fort Augustus and back into Inverness.

On 4 January 1934 the bubble began to show the first signs of its imminent disintegration when the Museum issued its report on the cast, compiled by Dr W. T. Calman, Keeper of Zoology, and M. A. C. Hinton, Deputy Keeper of Mammals. The learned gentlemen reported, somewhat huffishly:

We are unable to find any significant difference between these impressions and those made by the foot of a hippopotamus. The closest agreement is with the right hind foot of a mounted specimen, probably not quite full grown. By the courtesy of the Superintendent of the Zoological Gardens, it has been possible to take a cast of the impression made by the same foot of a living female.

In general character this impression also agrees with the Loch Ness footprints, but the impressions left by the fleshy portions of the sole are much fuller and more rounded than in the case of the dried mounted specimen or of the Loch Ness footprints.

The report caused red faces and an embarrassed shuffling of feet in one Fleet Street office and howls of laughter from all their rivals. The prints had, in fact, been made by the stuffed foot of a hippopotamus which was part of an umbrella stand owned by a Loch Ness resident. It is not clear to this day whether Mr Wetherall actually conspired with the young sons of the foot's owner to bring about the hoax or whether he too had been taken in by it.

Although this was not the only hoax perpetrated at the time (others moored barrels in the loch and built makeshift models), it was the one which received the greatest publicity and had the most detrimental effect on the animals' reputation. Through that facet of the human mind which retains comedy and humour more easily than hard fact, the hoaxes were remembered and the genuine sightings either forgotten or ignored. Scientists mopped their brows and breathed a 'Just as I thought' sigh and most newspapers adopted a steadily more cynical approach.

To make matters even worse, in the early hours of the morning of 5 January a man claimed he had seen one of the animals bounding across the new motor road (see Chapter 6). This really was too much, even for many sympathetic observers. The fact that the witness was a reliable young veterinary student was forgotten as people drew the excusable conclusion that this was yet another stunt.

For the *Daily Mail* expedition this new development was rather well timed, since it shifted an uncomfortably hot spotlight away from them. Messrs Wetherall and Pauli transferred their attentions to the place where the witness claimed the animal had passed. Strangely, three-toed footmarks, a heap of bones and a dead goat were shortly discovered. What is even stranger is that none of these things had been present when the witness had privately examined the area with members of his family earlier in the morning.

On 15 January Mr Wetherall claimed he saw one of the animals himself from the deck of the motor cruiser *Penguin*, chartered by the expedition. Unfortunately, everybody else on the boat happened to be looking in the wrong direction at the time. However, what he saw convinced him that Loch Ness contained a large grey seal and nothing more. The *Daily Mail* reported this as its conclusion and the expedition slipped unobtrusively away. The following year Mr Wetherall resigned his Fellowship of the Royal Geographical Society.

The story was beginning to die the death of all those that receive an excess of sudden publicity and do not live up to expectations. So far, despite the efforts of the world's press and many hundreds of enthusiastic visitors, all that existed was a very hazy still photograph and a few seconds of cine film showing a water disturbance. Hardly a very convincing performance by a 'Monster' with such a doting public.

Hoax or no hoax, Loch Ness had now been established as the home of a 'Monster'. It is frequently suggested by those who do not know any better that the whole thing was an invention by the local Tourist Board. Ironically it was an hotel-owner, as we have seen, who sparked it off and began the modern phase of the saga. However, although local businessmen were quick to cash in on the mystery there are simply no grounds for suggesting that they created it in the first place.

In February 1934, Inverness Town Council reduced its grant to the Highlands Advertising Board by one third because they considered the 'Monster' in itself to be sufficient publicity for the region. Mr A. F. MacKenzie, the Board's secretary, said: 'The district is hoping for a £10,000 summer season. It all depends on the Monster.' It appears they were not disappointed. At Easter the Royal Automobile Club reported that Loch Ness had outstripped the West Country in the number of requests for travel information and had become the most popular destination for motorists in Britain.

A new industry in souvenirs was created. Among the collection of Monster pincushions, tea-cosies and chocolate effigies was 'Sandy, the Loch Ness Monster – in three sizes – covered in green embossed velveteen and filled with Java kapok'. In London a famous restaurant served 'Le filet de sole Loch Ness'. In Massachusetts and Connecticut a new fashion in women's clothes was inspired by the animals. It was an ensemble called simply 'Loch Ness', consisting of a 'Slender dark green wool frock with a hip length jacket of the same fabric with long front tails furred in grey fox'.

*

Of all the evidence which has accumulated over the past forty years there is one photograph that has attracted more publicity and controversy than any other. It has become known simply as 'the Surgeon's Photograph' and is believed to be the only genuine picture of the head and neck of one of the animals.

The man who took the series of pictures which includes the famous photograph was Lieutenant Colonel Robert Kenneth Wilson, M.A., M.B., Ch.B.Camb., F.R.C.S., a gynaecologist who, when he took the photographs in April 1934, was practising in Queen Anne Street, just off Harley Street, London.

After the Second World War, during which he served in the Royal Artillery, Colonel Wilson and his family moved abroad and eventually settled in Australia, where he died in 1969. It is with the kind permission of his widow, Mrs Gwen Wilson, that a photograph of him is reproduced here, showing for the first time the man whose contribution to the saga was (unintentionally) so great and yet who for professional reasons always shunned all connection with it.

Because of this desire to avoid publicity, the circumstances of the taking of the photographs have never been entirely clear. However, by piecing together original letters from Colonel Wilson, information from his wife, and contemporary press accounts, it is possible to describe the events surrounding the photography.

Colonel Wilson and a Mr Maurice Chambers of Thornbury were the lessees of a wild-fowl shoot on the north shore of the Beauly Firth close to Inverness. Having a few days' leave in the spring of 1934, Colonel Wilson and a friend decided to travel north to visit the shoot and take some photographs of wild fowl and trains. Accordingly, he borrowed a quarter-plate camera fitted with a telephoto lens.

On the day in question, in early April, they were driving northwards along the new motor road above Loch Ness. At about 7 or 7.30 a.m., Colonel Wilson stopped the car about two miles north of Invermoriston on a small promontory, well studded with trees and about 100 feet above water level, next to a small stream. Colonel Wilson continues in a letter:

I had got over the dyke and was standing a few yards down the slope and looking towards the loch when I noticed a considerable commotion on the surface some distance out from the shore, perhaps two or three hundred yards out. I watched it for perhaps a minute or so and saw something break the surface. My friend shouted: 'My God, it's the Monster!'
I ran the few yards to the car and got the camera and then went down and along the steep bank for about fifty yards to where my friend was and got the camera focused on something which was moving through the water. I could not say what this object was as I was far too busy managing the camera in my amateurish way.

Colonel Wilson made four exposures in a space of about two minutes, by which time the object had completely disappeared.

44

'I had no idea at the time whether I had got anything on the plates or not. I only thought I might have,' he said.

As soon as they arrived in Inverness, Colonel Wilson took the four plates to Ogston's, a local chemist, where he gave them to Mr George Morrison to be developed. As he handed them in Colonel Wilson asked for particular care to be taken with them, at which Mr Morrison remarked: 'You haven't got the Loch Ness Monster, have you?' Colonel Wilson replied that he thought he might have. The plates were ready the same day. The first two were blank; the third, the famous one, showed an animal's upraised head and neck, and the last one showed the head disappearing into the water. On Mr Morrison's advice, Colonel Wilson sold the copyright of the best photograph to the *Daily Mail*, which published it on 21 April 1934, thereby challenging the evasive ingenuity of the scientific community yet again.

Colonel Wilson refused to enlarge upon the bare facts of his story and would not try to estimate the size of the object. In fact, he never claimed that he had photographed the 'Monster'; all he ever said was that he photographed an object moving in the waters of Loch Ness. He wrote: 'I am not able to describe what I saw. As I finished, the object moved a little and submerged.' However, his friend saw the animal clearly and described it in terms very similar to the appearances on the photographs.

The detached and entirely objective approach of Colonel Wilson is surely commendable. He made no wild claims and, as one would expect from a professional scientific man of standing, he merely reported what had happened as far as his recollection would allow him. Having done that he wished to have no part in the wrangling which inevitably follows every photograph purporting to show one of the animals.

The general climate of zoological opinion was of bewildered bafflement. Dr Calman of the Natural History Museum said he could not hazard a guess as to what it was. Others fell back on the 'tree root' theory.

In studying the two photographs it should be remembered that whereas photograph No. 2 shows the entire negative area, photograph No. 1 shows only a portion of the whole picture. The original negatives of both have now been lost. In addition, the quality of photograph No. 2 is very poor; the picture was clearly out of focus when it was taken, and light has clouded the right-hand side. However, despite these handicaps, a valid comparison is still possible.

The well-known photograph shows the characteristic long, graceful neck and small head, behind which is what may be part of the body just breaking the surface. Observers have speculated that the dark object just to the right of the neck might be the tip of a flipper. Of more significance is the pattern of ripples on the water surface. As Tim Dinsdale pointed out in his book *Loch Ness Monster* (Routledge and Kegan Paul, 1960; pages 68–77), there is clear evidence of a ring of concentric ripples spreading out around the neck and also another separate ring to the rear, behind the portion of 'body', which suggests another part of the animal just below the waterline.

The second photograph, which is taken from a print which Mr George Morrison kept from the original negative, shows the top of the neck and the head just before it submerged. Despite the hazy outline, one can clearly see the similarity between the two. The proportions are the same although the scale is different. This second picture, showing as it does the entire frame, shows that the photograph was taken from above the waterline and, most important, it proves that the object is not, as one scientist has continually suggested, the tail of an otter in the act of diving. If it had been, there would obviously have been no time for the photographer to have changed plates and taken a second photograph.

These are most valuable pictures. They have been rigorously scrutinized for any evidence of faking and no flaws have ever been found in them.

An interesting postscript to the story of the 'Surgeon's Photograph' is that in 1972 the better picture was submitted to the computer-enhancement process used by America's National Aeronautical and Space Administration (N.A.S.A.) on the *Apollo* moon photographs. This process greatly improves clarity by removing all the 'noise' in a photograph and enlarges it without losing the area between grains. The improved picture showed definite signs of 'whiskers' hanging down from the animal's lower jaw and must finally remove any lingering doubts about the authenticity of this photograph.

Three months after Colonel Wilson took his photographs the first serious investigation of any size to resolve the mystery was launched. Its sponsor was Sir Edward Mountain, Chairman of the Eagle Star and British Dominions Insurance Company. He had taken Beaufort Castle near Beauly for the summer of 1934 and was soon attracted by the events at Loch Ness. Being an enterprising businessman with a healthy curiosity he decided to finance a photographic expedition to the loch.

With the help of his firm's publicity manager and Captain James Fraser of Inverness, who was placed in overall charge of the expedition, twenty unemployed men were signed up from the Inverness labour exchange. On their insurance cards they all entered their occupations as 'Watchers for the Monster', which was duly registered by the Department of Health.

Each man was supplied with a pair of binoculars and a Kodak box camera. They were paid £2 per week, with a bonus of ten guineas for anyone who took a successful photograph. Two coaches were hired which, for the five weeks from 13 July, brought the men out from Inverness at 8 o'clock every morning. Fourteen men were positioned along the northern shore and six along the southern. They watched from their stations each day until 6 p.m., when they were taken back into Inverness to report to the press waiting at the Eagle Star offices.

During the course of the expedition a total of eleven reasonably clear sightings were made and several photographs were taken. One of the best sightings was made by Mr P. Grant at about 10.45 a.m. on 12 August from Abriachan Pier. In his daily report he wrote:

I saw the object appear in the water about 120 yards from the shore. I had no glasses or camera but was able to make out clearly the monster's head which appeared to be like that of a goat. On top of the head were two stumps resembling a sheep's horns broken off. The neck was about 40 inches long and where neck and body met appeared considerable swelling which resembled a fowl with a full crop. The colour of the body was between nigger and dark brown and appeared to be lighter underneath. The skin appeared to be smooth, the markings were like that of a lizard. The animal appeared to have flippers on the fore part of the body and these were extended straight forward and were not being used. The eyes appeared to be mere slits like the eye of a darning needle. I watched the creature for about five minutes then it submerged. It was moving at a speed of about 8 m.p.h., and there was no wash or commotion in the water, but after it had disappeared air bubbles appeared at the front and the rear. Length of the body was 20 ft.

Of the five photographs taken which showed anything, four show water disturbances which can clearly be attributed to passing boats. The fifth, reproduced here with the permission of Sir Edward's son, Sir Brian Mountain, is more interesting since it shows an isolated dark object with what appears to be spray being thrown up on one side of it. The picture quality is poor and the object is hazy, but it does at least suggest the presence of something large in the water.

The greatest success of the expedition was achieved by Captain Fraser himself. After five weeks the watchers were laid off and Captain Fraser, the first true 'Monster-hunter', and one assistant kept up the watch. At about 7.15 a.m. on the morning of 15 September Captain Fraser took up his position below the road above and just north of Urquhart Castle. This, in his own words, is what happened:

I was looking northwards when I noticed something in the water about three quarters of a mile away, just out of Urquhart Bay. I could not recollect a rock being there so raised my binoculars and studied it. There was a slight heat haze which did not make things very clear but I could see a dark object in the water. The only thing I could describe it as being like is an upturned, flat-bottomed boat. It must have been about 15 feet long and was dark in colour.

I thought I might as well shoot some film so put the cine camera to my eye, pressed the button and fortunately it started to operate. I filmed it for about two minutes and then something came up out of the water, there was a spume of spray and it disappeared.

The film was packed and dispatched to London by train, where members of the Kodak staff met it and developed it. The camera Captain Fraser had used was a 16mm. Kodak cine with

48

a six-inch telephoto lens. The film was soon viewed by zoologists who by now had apparently decided that strength would lie in unity since, with very few exceptions and for no apparent scientific reason, they stated that the object was a seal.

At a meeting of the Linnaean Society in London the seal theory was expounded with greater confidence, although one member suggested that it might be an otter. Commander Gould, who spoke at the meeting, repeated a remark made to him during his own field inquiries that London scientists seemed to think that Highlanders were all half-witted and did not know a seal when they saw one. Actually, of course, many of them saw more seals in a month than most Londoners do in their whole lives. Sir Edward Mountain wrote after the meeting: 'The scientists would have been much wiser to say that they did not know what it was. To say, as some did, that it was a seal and that the head and neck (if seen!) belonged to something else was to say the least, a pity.'

Meanwhile, as the men of learning in London winced and grunted, Captain Fraser was continuing his vigil. When I met him by the lochside in the summer of 1973 he recounted some of the experiences of his watch, many of which are indicative of the general atmosphere and attitude to the mystery back in 1934. Among his many recollections he described how, at one time, there were nearly 200 cars drawn up on the road behind him, their occupants lined up, straining their eyes and following his every movement. 'I would turn to the right and they would all turn to the right. I would point to something and near pandemonium would break out – it was the funniest thing you could imagine!'

He went on to describe how one day two large cars drew up and a group of people descended into the field to meet him. Among them was an alderman from a large English city.

He asked me when it was going to come up and I replied: 'Any moment now.' He looked at his watch and said that they would wait for an hour. After the hour had passed and nothing had appeared he came up to me greatly agitated and said: 'You know I could have you imprisoned for getting people here under false pretences.'
Well, of course, at first I thought he must be joking, but he wasn't

– he was deadly serious. I told him he didn't have to come and he became very indignant and stormed off.

I asked Captain Fraser whether he suffered much ridicule. He replied that he did, particularly from British visitors. 'They just looked upon it as the biggest joke of the century. There was far greater interest from foreigners, particularly Americans.' Two of his visitors, he recalled, had come all the way from Australia just to spend a few days at Loch Ness. 'On another occasion I met an American with a copy of a New York newspaper. In England at the time the big news was the launching of the Queen Mary. This was pictured in the American paper but, in comparison, there were four pages devoted to "Latest Loch Ness Monster Sightings".'

One British person who was interested in the expedition was King George V. He twice made inquiries about the progress of Sir Edward's team, and members of the Royal Family visited the loch on several occasions.

At about this time a Paris newspaper reported that the 'Monster' was really a German airship which had fallen into the loch during the last war. In response, a War Office spokesman was attributed with the ambiguous statement: 'The whole thing is ridiculous.' Four years later a party of Germans were to claim that they had captured the 'Monster' and spirited it secretly out of the country and that it was on display in Bavaria. Mr John Young, a seventy-year-old gravedigger from Lewiston, used a telephone for the first time in his life in June 1934 to tell the press that he had seen one of the creatures. 'I always thought it was a bit of a joke, but now I am convinced it is true,' he said. 'I was walking along the road beside Urquhart Castle when the beast came up. It had a long neck and a small head. It was very big.'

In November 1935 'Nessie' was blamed for giving Inverness a name for bad drinking habits. Ex-Provost Petrie said: 'The town has a bad reputation for strong drink, not through any fault of ours, but through the Loch Ness Monster, because any time it is alleged to have been seen people attribute it to strong drink!' In May 1934 a London opera correspondent reported in disgust about 'an audible murmur in the Covent Garden auditorium when the dragon came on to be slain in *Siegfried* last night. First of all, people began to whisper what sounded like "Loch Ness Monster", followed by disapproving sounds.' Later the same year a motion picture entitled *The Secret of the Loch* was shot on location starring Seymour Hicks.

Commander Rupert Gould's book, published in the summer of 1934, enjoyed a mixed reception. Among the more hostile critics some tried to cast doubts on his sanity and integrity. Dr W. T. Calman wrote in the *Spectator*:

There is no need to question that all of them [fifty-eight witnesses who reported sightings between May 1933 and May 1934] saw something unusual in the familiar surroundings of the loch; but there is a possibility that neither they nor Commander Gould fully realise how easily and inevitably recollections of things seen become tinged and distorted by previous and even by subsequent impressions.

It is only fair to note that Commander Gould embarked on his inquiries fully aware of the shortcomings of the human power of recollection and with no anticipation that they 'would lead to any surprising conclusions'.

By the end of 1934 the mystery had more or less exhausted its potential as a subject for prolonged media coverage, although its visitor-pulling power was undiminished. Sightings continued, but unless they were of exceptional interest they would usually be ignored by all but the local press.

In August 1938 a private party of twenty adventurers announced that they were to set off to Loch Ness to kill and capture the 'Monster' with harpoons, guns, speedboats and nets. Fortunately their plans were dropped when the local police and the Fishery Board stepped in. This provoked a fresh demand for official legal protection for the animals. The case of Pelorus Jack, a huge grampus which for many years around the turn of the century used to pilot ships through Cook Strait, New Zealand, was quoted as a precedent; he had been protected by an Order in Council of the New Zealand Government. The British Government, however, refused to show similar sentiment, and no law or official order was passed. Nevertheless, the animals were not entirely ignored by the courts. During a case on whale oil in the Court of Appeal in 1938, when one of the judges was trying to discover whether whales are to be found in the Arctic, his colleague Lord Justice Greer offered the helpful advice 'You might find one in Loch Ness!'

The year 1938 also saw the attempted launching of another serious expedition. Captain D. J. Munro, R.N., proposed establishing a company, 'Loch Ness Monster Ltd', with blocks of one-shilling shares. He estimated it needed £1,500 to finance the scheme, which involved setting up three fixed camera stations on the loch shore, each manned by 'One naval officer in charge of trained observers. One marine (private) or blue-jacket and two others.' Captain Munro stated: 'No dividend can be expected. At the same time if good shots are obtained by the cameras the results may be most valuable.' Sadly the scheme never materialized, since only £90 was forthcoming. It was to be a quarter of a century before a similar scheme was operated at Loch Ness.

A few more photographs and films were taken in the years before the war. On 10 June 1934 a group of Morayshire holidaymakers had a sighting near Fort Augustus, and a photograph was taken showing a long, dark object on the surface. The woman who took the picture said:

We were always doubtful about the truth of any Monster existing in Loch Ness, but now I have no doubt that there is some living thing in the loch which scientists have not yet been able to explain. I happened to gaze across the loch and I was amazed to see an object slowly come to the surface. It made very little commotion.

I cried: 'Look, it's the Monster,' and took a snap with my little camera. Then it swam for a few yards and disappeared. It was black, about 15 to 18 feet long and 200 yards or so away.

Mr Malcolm Irvine took another film on 22 September 1936 which he said showed one of the animals. He had been carrying on an intermittent search after taking his first film in December 1933, and although he had had several more brief sightings he had not had an opportunity to take any more film until he saw an unidentifiable object coming across the loch from Foyers. Describing the film he said: 'It shows the head and neck parallel with the surface and rising and falling with the movement of the huge body. The humps are also seen rising and falling gently

1. Aerial view looking north up Loch Ness from above Fort Augustus. (Aerofilms)
2. Aerial view looking south down Loch Ness from above Lochend. (Aerofilms)

3. The ruins of Castle Urquhart. (Nicholas Witchell)

4. Alex Campbell's report of the Mackay sighting in the *Inverness Courier* which is credited with having started the 'Monster' mystery. (*Inverness Courier*)

HIGHLAND ORPHANAGE

wn Council's Confidence in the Trustees

JECTIONS TO SCHEME

night, at the monthly meeting of the rness Town Council, it was unanimously ed to oppose the draft scheme of the tion Endowments (Scotland) Com- a in regard to the government of the nd Orphanage.

vost Donald Macdonald, in moving the Council express their confidence e present Trustees and oppose the cheme, said everyone in the High- aired how the late Mr Walker, Mr Mr Cook had managed the High- tage, and how well it was now their sons. He thought it t shame if the government was interfered with. (Ap-

Macleod, in seconding pretent management oth the school and 're carried on in a not know of any hich was better hland Orphanage, sorry if any change nagement of the in-

e, in supporting the ouncil should use every p this dead hand off a He believed if the no change would take ment of the institution.

E TRUSTEES:

from Mr Robert rd to the history o was read:—

nents (Scotland) n inquiring into the hland Orphanage, and a draft scheme for the Or- fich is exceedingly objection- Trustees of the Orphanage, and, also be very objectionable to subscribe to it. I have been ur attention to the matter, ur assistance to see that on is not allowed to

narriage was founded ot and the late Mr ds they were joined and they gradually ye as it at present nerally from 75 to t Trustees are the

---

STRANGE SPECTACLE ON LOCH NESS

What was it?

(FROM A CORRESPONDENT).

Loch Ness has for generations been credited with being the home of a fearsome-looking monster, but, somehow dr other, the "water- kelpie," as this legendary creature is called, has always been regarded as a myth, if not a joke. Now, however, comes the news that the beast has been seen once more, for, on Friday of last week, a well-known business man, who lives near Inverness, and his wife (a University graduate), when motoring along the north shore of the loch; not far from Abriachan Pier, were startled to see a tremendous upheaval on the loch, which, previously, had been as calm as the proverbial mill-pond. The lady was the first to notice the disturbance, which occurred fully three-quarters of a mile from the shore, and it was her sudden cries to stop that drew her husband's attention to the water.

There, the creature disported itself, rolling and plunging for fully a minute, its body re- sembling that of a whale, and the water cas- cading and churning like a simmering caul- dron. Soon, however, it disappeared in a boiling mass of foam. Both onlookers con- fessed that there was something uncanny about the whole thing, for they realised that here was no ordinary denizen of the depths, because, apart from its enormous size, the beast, in taking the final plunge, sent out waves that were big enough to have been caused by a passing steamer. The watchers waited for almost half-an-hour in the hope that the monster (if such it was) would come to the surface again; but they had seen the last of it. Questioned as to the length of the beast, the lady stated that, judging by the state of the water in the affected area, it seemed to be many feet long.

It will be remembered that a few years ago, a party of Inverness anglers reported that when crossing the loch in a rowing-boat, they encountered an unknown creature, whose bulk, movements, and the amount of water it dis- placed at once suggested that it was either a very large seal, a porpoise, or, indeed, the monster itself!

But the story, which duly appeared in the press, received scant attention and less cre- dence. In fact, most of those people who aired their views on the matter did so in a manner that bespoke feelings of the utmost scepticism. It should be mentioned that, so far as is known, neither seals or porpoises have ever been known to enter Loch Ness. Indeed, in the case of the latter, it would be utterly im- possible for them to do so, and, as to the seals, it is a fact that though they have on rare occasions been seen in the River Ness, their presence in Loch Ness has never once been definitely established.

ANOTHER DARING INVERNESS BURGLARY

CORRESP

TO THE EDITOR OF

Sir,—May I crave columns to express m or harangue, which Co has made in your last justified protest again meeting of the Hi stead of replying to parent'y gone out of I think, a most unjus tack on the parties wh carious position of Hig dared to suggest that be formed so as to cn a sounder bar people not only wit Highland League "stooped by inst end by the dist shire Associati

Could a more against men, for i Angus Forbes, who real service for north Mr Lyon, the president word has always been these gentlemen joini two Leagues! They something to say ag The Aberdeenshire A to look after itself enlightened Inverr Councillor Fraser when he presumes the clubs who are to destroy the F carried.

Why, may I as northern clubs be a cock to teams from the Highland area? protest against his League meeting whi tried to explain away enter into a controve Fraser, who prates ab ledge of Highland footb to the test he has not ev to offer how to improve it and only gives a displa ness, which I venture t anybody. I desire to ball position put on so one with the slightest ditions of Highland that position will Peterhead and Fr matter, the othe shire Football L proper district. visualised "a hi position for Hig

TO THE F

5. Hugh Gray's photograph – the first which claimed to show the 'Monster'. (*Daily Record*, Glasgow)

6. One of the first 'monster-hunters' at the loch in the winter of 1933–4 rigging a flash camera triggered by a trip wire. (Associated Newspapers)

7. M. A. Wetherall (*left*), the big-game hunter engaged in December 1933 by the *Daily Mail*, with his cameraman, Gustave Pauli. (*The Times*)

8. Mr Wetherall examining the famous 'footprints' on the beach near Dores. (Associated Newspapers)

9. A police officer warns residents and visitors not to try to harm the animals (December 1933). (*The Times*)

10. A party of boy scouts sets off by boat to search for the 'Monster' in January 1934. (*The Times*)

11. A cage being prepared for shipment to Loch Ness in case one of the animals should be caught (December 1933). (*Glasgow Herald*)

12. A picture postcard, one of the many souvenirs produced on the Monster theme in the 1930s. (Valentines of Dundee)

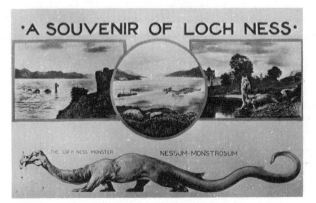

13. The famous 'Surgeon's Photograph', taken in April 1934, said to show one of the animals' upraised neck and head. (Associated Newspapers)

14. The final photograph taken by the Surgeon, showing the object disappearing into the water.

15. Colonel R. K. Wilson, the 'Surgeon'. (By courtesy of Mrs Gwen Wilson)

16. One of the photographs taken by Sir Edward Mountain's team of watchers in the summer of 1934, showing a dark shape with what appears to be spray being thrown up into the air. (By courtesy of Sir Brian Mountain)

17. Lachlan Stuart's photograph, taken in July 1951. (*Daily Express*)

18. The B B C Television floating control room for the programme
The Legend of the Loch (1958). (B B C)

19. BBC divers preparing to search for the 'Monster'. (*Courier and Advertiser*, Dundee)

20. The echo-sounder chart of the trawler *Rival III*, showing the unidentified contact.

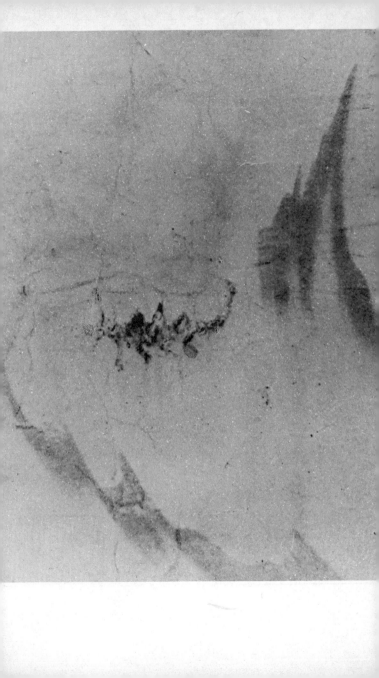

21. H. L. Cockrell's photograph, taken from a canoe early one morning in the summer of 1958. (Camera Press, London)

22. P. A. Macnab's photograph, taken in July 1955. Compare the size of the object in the water with Urquhart Castle tower, which is 64 feet high. (P. A. Macnab)

23. Peter Macnab.

24. Artist's reconstruction of the Grant land sighting. (Alan Jones)

25. Mr W. Arthur Grant, photographed shortly after he claimed his land sighting.

as the flippers move beneath them. It was over 30ft long and almost black in colour.'

After seeing the film, Mr Eric Foxon, a Fellow of the Linnaean Society which had displayed no enthusiasm for the subject two years earlier when shown Captain Fraser's film, said: 'The animal does not fall into any known category. The doubts of the sceptics are shattered. Henceforward everyone will require to admit that there is something in Loch Ness.'

His remark fell on deaf ears. The press and the establishment had become rather indifferent to the 'Monster' and were unwilling to risk further contact with it. They were all rather more inclined towards the view of Mr Boulenger of the London Zoo Aquarium: 'The whole business is a stunt foisted on a credulous public and only excused by a certain element of low comedy' (*Observer*, 1 July 1934).

The world was now having to focus its attention on that other monster who had shared the headlines with Nessie in 1933. The people of Europe began to prepare themselves for the coming holocaust and, as troops replaced tourists on the shores of Loch Ness, the comparative trivialities of 'monster-hunting' were temporarily forgotten.

Chapter Four

'Look – the Loch Ness Monster!'

In countries throughout the world the verbal testimony of a witness forms part of the fundamental basis of the judicial procedure. Until quite recently in Britain such testimony could have constituted sufficient evidence on which to have executed a person.* It has been calculated that there are over 4,000 people who believe they have seen an unknown animal in Loch Ness. Whatever proportion of these reports one can explain away in terms of dishonesty and genuine misinterpretation, there has always remained a substantial quantity, possibly only 15 to 20 per cent, which simply defy any attempt to dismiss them in terms of known animals and objects, hoaxes or fraudulent witnesses.

It is a puzzling reflection on our purportedly intelligent, rational society that the testimony of so many reliable witnesses, often offered under oath, should for so long have been considered inadequate as proof that there is something unknown in Loch Ness. The puzzle approaches absurdity when one studies the quality of many of the reports and the qualifications of the witnesses. Included in this chapter are the accounts of monks, lawyers, the sister-in-law of a British Prime Minister, a Nobel Prize winner, a Knight Commander, a Count, policemen, professional men of repute and many people experienced in loch observation. And this chapter represents only a tiny fraction of the total eye-witness evidence available.

It is, of course, right that the standards of scientific acceptance should be most stringent, but equally they must surely be sufficiently flexible to give way when overwhelming pressure is

* G. K. Chesterton once wrote: 'Many a man has been hanged on less evidence than there is for the Loch Ness Monster.'

placed on them. The reaction of the scientific community to the Loch Ness phenomenon has been sadly reminiscent of a remark made by Dr James Ritchie, Keeper of the Royal Scottish Museum's Natural History Department, who, on hearing that an unusual carcase had been washed up at Stronsay in 1808, said: 'There is no need to depend on the obscure descriptions of the house painters and crofters of Orkney which set the scientific world a-jingling.' Accordingly, none of them bothered to go north to examine what the local people believed to be the body of a sea-serpent.

Let us, therefore, move on and look at a sample of the most significant 'obscure descriptions' from Loch Ness and at the stars of this story – the animals themselves.

*

Alex Campbell has already been mentioned in connection with his report of the Mackay sighting in April 1933. A year later he himself had a sighting which has become one of the most well-known on account of his manifest sincerity and great experience of Loch Ness.

At about 9.30 on a calm May morning in 1934, Mr Campbell was standing on a promontory of land by the mouth of the River Oich in Fort Augustus looking across the loch towards Borlum Bay. Suddenly, 'a strange object seemed to shoot out of the calm waters almost opposite the Abbey boathouse.' When it came to rest about 600 yards away, Mr Campbell identified it as a large animal, the like of which he had never seen before. The head and neck stood about six feet out of the water. The neck was about one foot thick and the head the size of a cow's, but flatter. The body, a large rounded hump, was about thirty feet long. 'I gauged this carefully in my mind's eye by placing two ordinary rowing boats of fifteen-foot overall length end to end.'

The animal was very alert and kept turning its head from side to side. The cause of its nervousness became apparent when two small boats appeared at the mouth of the Caledonian Canal. As soon as they came into the animal's line of vision it dived, leaving a large turmoil of water.

During a lifetime spent in contact with Loch Ness, including forty-seven years as one of its water bailiffs, Mr Campbell has encountered the animals on a number of other occasions. On 16 July 1958 he saw two of them, again near Borlum Bay. One large black hump was heading diagonally towards the far side of the loch, churning the surface around it, while the other black hump was lying comparatively quietly near St Benedict's Abbey.

A couple of years previously Mr Campbell came into uncomfortably close contact with a solid object in the loch. He describes what happened:

It was a beautiful summer day in 1955 or 1956. I was out rowing my boat in the middle of the loch opposite the Horseshoe. Without any warning the boat started to heave underneath me. It was terrifying. My dog was with me in the boat – an Airedale terrier – and he leapt from where he was in the stern sheets to lie crouching and shivering under my seat. I was really scared – honest to goodness I was. It is the only time I have ever felt frightened on this loch in my whole life. I can't explain it – the boat just seemed to rise and then stagger back almost immediately. Believe me, I put my back into the oars to get away from that spot – I didn't even dare move to the stern to start the motor.

The reaction of fear on the part of the dog is interesting. Mr Campbell came across a similar animal display one day just before the last war when he visited a family of gypsies camped by the lochside near Point Clair. Earlier in the morning, he was told, the father of the family had been woken by the restlessness of a pony tethered nearby. He got up and was trying to quieten it when he looked out over the water and saw the cause of the animal's excitement. About forty yards from the shore was a creature with 'a huge black, swanlike neck raising and dipping into the water as it cruised slowly around.' Although it was several hours after the incident, Mr Campbell said the father was still visibly shaken by it.

On 17 June 1934 a group of members of the Inverness Scientific Society and Field Club saw one of the animals in mid-loch from near Abriachan. Amongst them were the ex-Provost of Inverness, David Petrie, Colonel E. G. Henderson, a member of Inverness Town Council, and Mr George MacBean, Registrar for the Burgh of Inverness. The coach in which they were travelling was pulled up when a big black object was noticed out in the water. At first they thought it might be a piece of debris, but this theory had to be discarded when they realized that it was travelling against the wind and waves. Ex-Provost Petrie later said 'It appeared to be a huge living creature.'

The animals seemed to favour people in authority in 1934, for on 8 August Inverness-shire's Member of Parliament, Sir Murdoch Macdonald, K.C.M.G. (a distinguished engineer who was a consultant in the construction of the Aswan Dam), saw one of them:

I set out with my son early from Inverness as I had an appointment with the Secretary of State in Portree at 10 a.m. There was not a ripple on the water. Between 6 a.m. and 7 a.m., as we reached a high point on the road about four miles short of Invermoriston, I saw something on the loch . . . we stopped and looked.

What we saw were two hummocks about equal in length and separated by a space equal to this length, the whole occupying about 15 feet, I should estimate. At first the creature was almost still but after a moment or two my son pointed out that it had a slow motion towards Fort Augustus. It caused no ripple and moved along about 100 yards in five minutes. We drove on until we were abreast of it; at this point a trailer was drawn up beside the road. We got out of the car and I banged on the door.

A man, a Yorkshireman judging by his accent, came out partly dressed and wondered what we wanted.

I said, 'Do you see that log on the water?' He turned round, hesitated, then threw up his arms in the greatest excitement, exclaiming, 'By Jove, the Monster!'

He then got out a small pair of binoculars. The colour of the animal was blackish grey and it was obviously not a tree-trunk or a boat. We saw no head nor tail. As a result of all this I was half an hour late for my appointment. Sir Godfrey said, 'Well, that's as good an excuse as any other.'

Going back a few months, we find that on 26 May 1934 Brother Richard Horan of St Benedictine's Abbey, Fort Augustus, had a very clear sighting. He was working near the Abbey boathouse when he heard a noise in the water. At first he did not bother to look up, but when he did so a few moments later he found one of the animals looking at him from a distance of about thirty yards. A graceful neck with a broad white stripe down its front stood about three and a half feet high at an angle of forty-five degrees to the water. He could not see any features on the head, although its muzzle appeared to be rather blunt and similar to a seal's. It moved about slowly until it found a rowing boat in its path, at which point it stopped momentarily and then swung round, causing a commotion in the water. Finally it plunged below the surface, and a mark similar to a torpedo track continued for a distance up the loch. This sighting was independently corroborated by three other people watching from a different position.

A somewhat similar sighting was reported on 22 December 1935 by a Miss Rena MacKenzie of Invermoriston.

It was about 3 p.m. when I saw it. Suddenly its head and neck rose from the calm surface of the loch and moved along quite near the shore. The head was small in comparison to the length and thickness of the creature's neck. What struck me most was that the under part of the neck was perfectly white. After about five minutes a passing steamer sounded its siren and the creature, after turning its head in an agitated manner, plunged out of sight.

The possibility of witness error or dishonesty and the hoary old 'mass hallucination' can surely be ruled out when a large group of unconnected people all testify to a sighting of one of the animals. This happened on the afternoon of 28 October 1936, when nearly fifty people from different cars and buses and from all walks of life stood on the roadside a mile and a half south of Urquhart Castle and watched a head, neck and two-hump display by one of the animals for nearly a quarter of an hour. The first person to see the animal was Mr Duncan MacMillan, from the door of his cottage situated above the road at Lennie. He saw a head and neck rise out of the water about 500 yards out in the loch, which was quite calm. Visibility was excellent and despite the distance Mr MacMillan had a clear view of the slowly moving object. He called to his wife, who joined him together with three visitors, his father and his wife's sister. As they stood and watched, two cars pulled up, followed by two coachloads of people and the local A.A. patrolman.

Mrs MacMillan described what then happened: 'Slowly the monster moved along with its head and neck clearly visible. The head was small and appeared to be greyish in colour. Then two distinct humps appeared, one of them fairly close to the head and the other some distance behind.'

A number of the travellers had telescopes and binoculars, and one witness described something to the rear of the second hump, just below the surface. This appeared to be moving from side to side and propelling the body. A few snapshots were taken but evidently with little success in view of the distance. However, nobody doubted that they were watching a large, living animal.

The following report is most unusual, since apart from enjoying a very clear view of one of the animals the witness also observed the creature apparently feeding. The report is taken from the 1 July 1938 issue of the *Inverness Courier*, a newspaper which has a consistent record for accurate reporting of sightings.

On Tuesday night Mr John MacLean, who belongs to Glen-Urquhart, saw the Loch Ness Monster from near the Halfway House Hotel, Invermoriston. Mr MacLean, who was standing at the shore near the mouth of the Altsigh Burn, watching to see whether any trout were rising, as he was contemplating fishing, said in an interview: 'In a moment I saw an extraordinary sight. It was the monster's head and neck less than twenty yards from me and it was without any doubt in the act of swallowing food. It opened and closed its mouth several times quite quickly and then kept tossing its head backwards in exactly the same manner as a cormorant does after it has devoured a fish.' What the monster had eaten Mr MacLean could not say, but at that particular spot the water teems with excellent trout.

But more interesting things were to follow. No sooner had the creature finished its meal than it dived below. Before it did so, however, two distinct humps and the entire length of the tail came to the surface. The animal then vanished head first but came up again a few yards further west, and there it lay for two to three minutes on top of the water, the tail again quite clear at the surface and both head and neck as well as two humps showing. In a moment or two it began to dive very slowly, and in doing so the head was submerged first, followed by the humps; but at this point the foremost hump became much larger and rose, in fact, almost twice as high out of the water as it had been at any time during its appearance. Summing up his description of the creature Mr MacLean said:

I was petrified with astonishment, and if I had had a camera with me I was so excited that I would probably have spoiled the chance of a lifetime. The monster, I am sure, is eighteen to twenty feet long, the tail fully six feet, and the largest hump was about three feet high. The head is small and pointed, the skin very dark brown on the back and like that of a horse when wet and glistening. The neck is rather thin and several feet long, but I saw no flippers or fins.

Miss Janet Fraser, who ran the Halfway House Hotel, confirmed that when Mr MacLean returned to the house immediately after the episode he appeared almost too overcome to tell her what had happened.

Sceptics frequently point to the shortcomings of the average person's ability to observe and report accurately as one of the main reasons for what, to them, is a misconceived belief that a living animal is responsible for the sightings. They rightly point out that virtually no two witnesses to a crime or an accident will ever describe exactly the same facts. And yet it is these very discrepancies in points of detail which give weight and substance to the reports. However, when it comes to Loch Ness sightings discrepancies are often taken as a sign of weakness and even of fraudulence. It is natural that different witnesses should report things in different ways and notice their own unique features. The discrepancies between eye-witness accounts show that people do not just imitate what others have reported in the past.

However feeble most of us may be at judging distance, size and speed and knowing the difference between an oil-drum and a 'monster', there are those who are trained to observe. One such group is the Royal Observer Corps, and during the Second World War members of the R.O.C. were stationed around Loch Ness. It is said that several members saw the animals but were forbidden to report the fact because of military discipline.

One member, however, did make his sighting known to a close friend. At 5.15 a.m. on 25 May 1943, Mr C. B. Farrel, while on duty at Fort Augustus, saw an unidentified object on the loch. When he looked through his binoculars (Zeiss × 6) he saw a creature twenty-five to thirty feet long about 250 yards away. In colour it appeared to be dark olive brown on top and lighter underneath. Its eyes seemed to be large, and the neck was described as being graceful and four to five feet in length. It was evidently feeding, since it kept depressing its head and neck until they were submerged and then it would quickly withdraw them from the water and shake its head vigorously. In the end the whole body slid out of sight without causing any disturbance.

The Deputy Lord Lieutenant of Inverness-shire is Mr William Mackay, D.L., O.B.E., F.S.A. He is also the Chieftain of the Glen Urquhart Games and used to be Dean of the Faculty of Lawyers in Inverness. Throughout his life he has led an active outdoor existence, which has included two sightings of the animals. At his home in the beautiful Strath Glass, near Loch Ness, he gave me this account:

The first time I saw the so-called Loch Ness Monster was in 1937. I was driving some boys back from Fort Augustus after a cricket match, and between Temple Pier and Abriachan I said in fun: 'Ten shillings to the boy who sees the Monster first.' A few minutes later we came round a corner and all the boys suddenly shouted at once: 'The Monster.' And there it was – two dark humps about three feet high, stationary in the water. We all got out and another three or four cars stopped too. Unfortunately I had to hurry on into Inverness but some of the boys in another car who remained saw it put up a long neck with a small head.

The next time Mr Mackay saw it, he told me, was just before the end of the last war. He was driving home from Foyers one evening when, about six hundred yards away across the loch opposite Urquhart Bay, he saw the same two humps again. He went on:

Fortunately this time I had my deerstalking telescope with me and so I stopped and examined the 'monster' through my glass. It appeared to be about thirty feet long in all, with a long neck which

61

it kept flat on the water. There were two humps which were dark elephant grey in colour. It looked as though there was hair over its back and body. The wind was from the west and the beast seemed to be trying to keep its head on to the wind, because every now and then I saw splashes and a long tail appeared to be sculling and two flippers to be paddling to change its position. Before I left, a Mr Deans, a plumber, drove up and told me that he too had been watching the animal.

A sighting which was to be of some significance was made on 4 April 1947. The witnesses were Mr J. W. McKillop, C.B.E., County Clerk of Inverness-shire, his son Mr Norman McKillop, an Edinburgh architect, an English friend, Mr Kenneth Cottier, and Mr John C. Mackay, chief reporter on the *Inverness Courier*. Mr J. W. McKillop gave his account of what happened:

We had left Inverness by motor car to go to Oban. After less than twenty minutes' driving, when we were about a mile north of Drumnadrochit, I saw a long wake on the water. I stopped the car and all the party rushed to the side of the loch and watched the wake growing larger. I then observed a very large moving object at the head of what I thought was foam. It was travelling at a very high speed and one of the party thought it might be a motorboat, but that idea was soon dispelled, for there was no sound at all. The large leading object continued to move quickly. I watched it very carefully for four or five minutes and my only regret was that I had not taken my binoculars with me. Only the head and part of a black body were visible and the rest apparently was covered by the water.

I had no doubt that there was something abnormal in the loch and that it must be the monster or some unusually big living object which was making one of its rare appearances. Soon the head disappeared but the trail was visible for some time before it too disappeared.

When Mr Cottier was interviewed this was the account he gave:

I had heard much about the Loch Ness Monster and was delighted to learn that our motor journey was by way of Loch Ness, all the more because it was a bright and sunny day. To my surprise the great loch was as calm as a pond, not a ripple on its broad expanse, and the sun almost in summer mood. The car stopped suddenly at a rise at the side of the loch and Mr McKillop shouted that there was something unusual in the loch.

We unmistakably sighted on the placid surface of the loch a fairly long slipstream which quickly developed in length, at the head of which were what seemed to be two shiny humps, close together, of which the first was the larger. The rapidity with which this exhaust-like stream in the wake of the two humps lengthened led me to believe that it might be a boat but for the fact that, it being a perfectly calm, clear day, any sound of a motorboat engine (for only a motorboat could have travelled at this speed) would be quite distinctly heard. Having such a clear view I observed that what was moving must be of considerable dimensions to make such a stir in the water.

The possibility of its being a motorboat was, as he added, entirely ruled out when the object and then the wake disappeared from the surface. Mr John Mackay said: 'The dark, high head was clearly seen. There can be no denial by even the most rabid scoffer – many of whom have never seen the loch – that in Loch Ness there is something abnormal – something larger than the usual species of marine animal.'

The sequel to this sighting was that at the next meeting of Inverness County Council the standing orders were suspended so that Mr McKillop could tell his colleagues about his 'glimpse of the most notorious inhabitant of the County'. One member remarked that 'Everybody knew that whatever the Chief Administrative Officer of the County said would be true. They would trust Mr McKillop's eyes better than their own.' The *Inverness Courier* reported the meeting as follows:

'I confess,' he [Mr McKillop] said, 'that I had certain doubts about it myself but these were largely removed by the fact that several men on whose word I could place reliance had seen the object. But any doubts that remained were completely dispelled on the afternoon of Good Friday when I had the good fortune to witness what is regarded as the Loch Ness Monster.

'I am firmly convinced there is something quite abnormal in the depths of the loch. It is capable of quite extraordinary speed and is capable of creating a commotion, a disturbance in the water that would suggest it must be of immense proportions.'

63

The meeting's Convenor, Lochiel, said that they were indebted to Mr McKillop for his statement.

'I was a great sceptic myself,' declared Lochiel, 'until I heard that Mr McKillop had seen it. I am quite convinced now there is a monster in Loch Ness. There could be no more trustworthy witness than our County Clerk.' (Applause)

Rev. Mr Graham: 'Nobody would believe me.' (Laughter) 'They would not even believe me when I said I saw it from a tearoom and not from an hotel.' (Laughter) Mr F. W. Walker said the 'Monster' should be made an honorary member of the County Council. Lochiel replied, amid laughter, 'that there was no provision for that in the Local Government Act.'

On the warm spring afternoon of 19 April 1950 Lady Maud Baillie, C.B.E., Commander of the A.T.S. during the last war and sister-in-law of Mr Harold Macmillan (later the British Prime Minister), was driving along the Dores to Foyers road with Lady Spring-Rice, wife of a former British Ambassador to the United States, and Lady Maud's grandsons, Angus and Jonathan Warr, and Lady Spring-Rice's grandson and granddaughter. Lady Maud described to me recently what happened:

I had just pointed out Urquhart Castle to the children when one of them asked 'Is that a rock out there?' I glanced across the water and saw something about one third of the way across the loch. I knew immediately that it could not be a rock that far out, so I pulled the car in to the side of the road. Just as I did so the 'rock' moved off at a very rapid pace in a northerly direction and after a few seconds it was concealed by the roadside vegetation. We all hurried down to the water's edge but the object had gone. But it had left a terrific wash which soon hit the shore with some violence and caused one of the children to run back in horror. What greatly impressed us all was the speed of the object and the great commotion it caused. Lady Spring-Rice said the wash was big enough to have been put up by a powerful speedboat. Although none of us saw it for long enough to give any real details, we all saw two separate big dark humps in the water. There was no question that it was a very large living animal.

Lady Maud, who has lived very near to the loch since the 1930s, went on to tell me about an occasion when she was asked by an old lady at her club in Edinburgh whether she was the person who had seen the 'Monster':

I replied that yes, I was, and asked her if she had ever seen it. To my surprise she said that she had, three times in one afternoon. I asked her to tell me about it and she described how a friend had once offered her a motor tour of the Great Glen so long as she did not bore her with silly remarks about a mythical 'Monster'. She promised that she would never mention it and the two of them set off. They were approaching Drumnadrochit in the car when this old lady saw one of the animals appear in the water below, but she remained silent and just watched it keep pace with them for a little while until it submerged. A moment later it resurfaced and this time the driver, who was the sceptic, saw it and said 'Good heavens, there's the Monster,' at which the old lady said 'Oh yes, I saw it a moment ago but didn't tell you because you made me promise not to mention it.' The two of them apparently watched it surface once more and then disappear for good. She didn't give any details of its appearance, but they were both quite convinced that it was the 'Monster'.

Lady Maud also provided evidence that some of the old Highland superstition about the animals still lingers on. She told me how a few years earlier her son had noticed a disturbance in the loch whilst out looking for deer on the estate above their home: 'He studied the area with his spyglass but didn't see anything break the surface. He then handed his glass to the keeper who was with him and said that there was something queer going on down the loch. But the keeper looked at him and refused to take the glass. He just said: "Aye, there's many a queer thing in that loch," and walked on.'

On 8 October 1958 a party of twenty-seven passengers on a bus watched a twenty-five-foot-long dark hump on the loch surface. Several of the witnesses broadcast an account of what they saw on the BBC Home Service on 16 October. They were interviewed by a BBC journalist, Mr Andy Cowan Martin, who added his own experience to the programme. This is his story as broadcast (reproduced by courtesy of the BBC):

It was a day in the month of June, way back in 1939, and I was flying from Kirkwall to Inverness and, just for fun, the pilot said he would take us over Loch Ness and we might see the Monster. We flew down the loch as far as Fort Augustus and on the way back I actually saw the Monster for about half a minute or so, but by the time I'd yelled to the other people in the plane to look where I was pointing and the pilot had brought the plane down nearer the surface of the loch, the Monster – the thing – giant eel or whatever it was, had submerged and all that the others could see was a swirl of foam. Frankly they didn't believe me when I said that for a few seconds I had a clear view of two very prominent sort of humps and a third one that was not so prominent and it looked something like the head of a seal.

Very few people carry either a camera or a pair of binoculars with them as they go about their daily business. This fact is one of several reasons why there are so few photographs of the animals. The residents of Loch Ness are far more likely to carry a telescope with them than a camera. Mr William Mackay studied the animal he saw through a glass; so did Mr Peter MacMillan, the head gamekeeper of the Glenmoriston estate, in August 1954. Mr MacMillan was working near the mouth of the River Moriston when a heavy wash hit the shore and made him look up. He saw two humps moving across the loch at speed and putting up waves 'like a speedboat'. He focused a powerful telescope on the humps and could see that they were part of a large animal. The skin was rough and similar to that of an elephant. The visible parts were about thirty feet in length.

On Sunday 16 June 1957 Mr D. Campbell, a native of Inverness and for thirty-two years the headmaster of Aldourie Public School, was walking across the low hills at the loch's northern end. He had sat down to read when he happened to look down at the loch and noticed what he took to be two boats which had suddenly appeared. They were about three quarters of a mile away and were travelling towards Urquhart Castle at a distance of about 150 yards from each other. Mr Campbell recollects that he wondered at the unusual course being taken by the 'boats' and also at the absence of any sign of people or oars. Then, quite suddenly, the left-hand object 'shot' across and stopped a little way to the right of the other one. Then they both sank out of sight. This account is valuable since it is one of the comparatively few which describe more than one animal on the surface at the same time.

In 1952 Dr Richard Synge was awarded the Nobel Prize for Chemistry. Fourteen years earlier, in the summer of 1938, he was staying at Fort Augustus with his parents and sisters when he saw one of the animals in Loch Ness. This is how he described what happened: 'It was about 8 o'clock one morning when I saw a dark hump-like object in the loch, which after a while started to move northwards close to the west bank of the loch. We all followed it by car for about three miles. It was going at a fair speed and leaving a slight wake, about a quarter of a mile from the shore. It then became stationary and then submerged.'

At about 4.20 p.m. on 2 February 1959 Automobile Association patrolman Mr Hamish Mackintosh was making a routine road report call to his office from the AA box at Brackla. As he finished he turned and looked out across the water and saw 'something out of this world. It was as if a dinosaur had reared up out of the loch.' A few hundred yards out was a tall, thin neck and a 'broad and very big' humped body, moving slowly towards the Brackla shore. The head and neck, which seemed to be towering about eight feet above the water, were greyish in colour and were turning from side to side. Mr Mackintosh was joined by a man from a nearby house, and both of them watched its slow progress for about five minutes. A fire engine went past but although they tried to wave it down it did not stop. However, a moment later two lorries did pull over and three more men joined the group. One of the most astonishing things, Mr Mackintosh said, was the way in which the animal submerged – it just sank perpendicularly without any commotion. After the event Mr Mackintosh declared that he would never again venture out on to Loch Ness in a small boat.

However, in 1963 four people did go on to the loch in a small boat – to chase after one of the animals and make one of the most exciting of all sightings at Loch Ness.

At about 7.30 on a still August evening, Mr Hugh Ayton and his son Jim were working in a field on their Balachladaich Farm, situated on the lochside about two miles south of Dores.

With them was another local farmer, Mr Alastair Grant, and a holidaymaker from Stirling, Mr Fred Gerrard, with his son Barry. This is the account Mr Ayton gave me:

My son was working with me in a field overlooking the loch when he looked up and saw something moving south about halfway across the loch. He shouted and the others ran up, and all five of us watched this thing moving down the loch. It was big and black and I realized that after fifteen years of farming here, at last I was actually watching the 'Monster'. The loch was calm and everything was quiet; there wasn't a noise anywhere – just this thing moving steadily forward. It was eerie, it really was.

Anyway we decided that the best thing would be to get the boat out and try to intercept it. So we all ran down to the jetty and four of us got into a rowing boat and set off. At first we rowed a short distance but then we started the little outboard motor.

The thing was still coming down the loch and as we got closer we could see more details of it. There was a long neck coming about six feet out of the water and a head which reminded me rather of a horse, though bigger and flatter. The body was made up of three low humps – about thirty to forty feet long in all, and about four feet high. The colour was dark and the skin looked rough. We must have got to within about fifty yards of it and then it rose up a little out of the water and dived and put up an enormous disturbance which swirled the boat around. A moment later the head appeared for a second a little further on and then it was gone for good.

In all it must have travelled about a mile, going at a steady pace all the time. At no time did we see any paddles or flippers.

The one feature of it that I'll always remember was the eye – an oval-shaped eye near the top of its head. I'll always remember that eye looking at us.

One of the animals exposed itself for an aristocratic inspection on 28 September 1966. Count Emmanuel de Lichtervelde of Belgium was being driven around the loch by Mr Guy Senior, Chairman of Inverness Unionist Association, and his wife. A few miles south of Dores they spotted a large dark object moving slowly along the loch. Mr Senior, a former naval officer, said: 'We stopped the car and watched the object for about six minutes. There were two distinct humps travelling at about eight knots but not causing much disturbance. It was definitely an animal we saw and very big. It could not possibly have been a boat or a wake caused by any vessel in the water.'

Count Lichtervelde was reported as saying: 'It was the most wonderful thing that could ever have happened to me. Nobody will believe me when I return to Belgium and say I have seen the famous "Monster".'

The most convincing testimonies often come from those who previously doubted the existence of the animals. Until a mid-April day of 1967 Mrs Dorothy Fraser, who lives in a cottage high on the hillside overlooking the loch at Achnahannet, was such a person. This is her story, which, even in print, conveys much of the colourful vivacity of its teller:

I was out in the garden and just thinking what a glorious day it was when all of a sudden I saw something come up gently out of the loch. It was a big, grey-black oval mass. I was so absolutely flabbergasted that I went weak at the knees. The first thing that came to my mind was that it was a submarine. 'Russians,' I said to myself, and looked for the periscope. Then it began to move, the penny dropped and I felt even more weak at the knees. After all these years when I've pooh-poohed the idea to scores of visitors, it was 'Nessie' herself.

It moved out to the centre of the loch, gently at first, and then it gathered speed until it was going quite fast, and then, as suddenly as it came, it sank, just like a porpoise going down. All that was left was a wake, and you could have said it was from a paddle-steamer, the waves were so big.

Although I am high up here and it must have been about quarter of a mile down and away from me, I had an excellent grandstand view. It must have been very big to have been so clear at that distance. It reminded me of the back of a huge giant tortoise.

Now I'm a firm believer. There is a lot of ridicule, but all one can do is tell the truth and hope that in the end everyone will realize that it *is* the truth.

It may have been noticed from the foregoing that the majority of the sightings have taken place when the loch was calm. This characteristic runs through about ninety per cent of all known sightings and perhaps suggests that the animals favour calm water for their surface appearances. Alternatively, it may simply be that they are easier to see when the loch surface is not broken up by waves. For instance, the following surfacing by one of the animals would have gone unnoticed had there not been a boat nearby.

On 16 March 1967 Mr John Cameron, a lock-keeper employed on the Caledonian Canal at Fort Augustus, was out salmon-fishing in his boat opposite Glendoe Pier. There was a stiff easterly wind and a three-foot wave on the loch. At about 3 p.m. Mr Cameron watched in astonishment as a large 'upturned boat' shaped object surged through the water, against the waves and wind, just twenty yards away from him and disappeared. It was about twelve feet in length, dark brown in colour, and had a crinkly surface. Mr Cameron told an *Inverness Courier* reporter: 'Believe me, it must be a very large animal as I saw only a part of it, and a powerful animal at that. You should have seen the way it sliced through the waves, quite effortlessly.'

Until about 11.45 a.m. on 22 June 1971 Mr William Dewar, a draughtsman from Lanarkshire, was among those who are sceptical about the existence of the 'Monster'. However, as he and his wife drove towards Fort Augustus on the A82, his doubts were shattered as his wife suddenly exclaimed 'Look, it's the Loch Ness Monster!' Three hundred yards away in the smooth water below them was a creature with a 'snake-like' head and neck moving quite rapidly in a southerly direction. About four feet behind the neck was a ten-foot-long dark hump standing two to three feet out of the water. After about a minute the animal submerged, leaving a bewildered and very excited couple standing by the roadside.

On successive days in October 1971 the animals were seen by a number of people, including a police inspector, a police sergeant and a monk. Tim Dinsdale records these sightings in the latest edition of his book *Loch Ness Monster* and writes of them: 'I realised that in this trilogy of witnesses' reports there might be found the key to modern credibility. No one could honestly doubt such people, or their ability to describe what they had seen.'

On 13 October, Police Inspector Henry Henderson and Police Sergeant George Mackenzie, both from Inverness, were among a group of people who watched two humps move up the loch near Altsigh Youth Hostel. The total length was estimated at thirty to forty feet, the speed at ten to fifteen m.p.h. Inspector Henderson wrote in a report: 'It was obvious that the two objects were part of one large animate object.' The next morning, 14 October, Father Gregory Brusey of the Fort Augustus Abbey was walking by the lochside below the Abbey with a friend, Mr Roger Pugh of London. 'Suddenly there was a terrific commotion in the waters of the bay. In the midst of this disturbance we saw quite distinctly the neck of the beast standing out of the water to what we calculated later to be a height of about ten feet. It swam towards us at a slight angle and after about 20 seconds slowly disappeared' (*Loch Ness Monster*, page 152).

Many of Father Brusey's colleagues at the Abbey have seen the creatures at one time or another. Father Aloysius Carruth, M.A., who has followed the mystery closely since the 1930s, and has written a small booklet on the subject (published by the Abbey Press, Fort Augustus), saw a large dark object proceeding up the centre of the loch early one morning in 1965. His brother, the Very Reverend Msgr G. E. Carruth, had a good sighting of the head, neck and humps in 1940.

*

Every year the sightings continue. On the evening of 27 July 1973 five people stood in the drive of the Foyers Hotel and watched one of the animals swim across the loch at speed. One witness, Mr J. Shaw of London, wrote: 'It is said that "seeing is believing", and we are now of the opinion that something exists in that loch.' Another witness, Mr E. J. R. Moran of Yorkshire, said: 'I can assure you now that although I was a sceptic before, now I don't mind what anyone thinks – I am convinced that I have seen a creature of some kind in Loch Ness.'

And so it goes on – just as it has for the past forty-odd years. Each time it happens somebody else shakes their head as a chimerical paper image gives way to a living creature of flesh and blood. The rich and the poor, the proud and the humble – they all stand and watch in self-effacing amazement as a legend comes to life before their eyes!

Chapter Five

Curiouser and Curiouser

The period from the Second World War to the late 1950s, when a new book on the subject appeared, was rather an uninspiring one for the Loch Ness mystery. It was always lurking in the background, and occasionally it would pop up in the news and create a fresh flutter of excitement. But no major progress was made. It became a classic 'hoary old chestnut' – dragged out every summer for a new feature article going over the old ground, cracking the old jokes and finishing with the usual question marks.

However, the period had its highlights. The animals' fatal attraction for those in the information industry even reached as far as Josef Goebbels, Nazi Germany's Minister of Propaganda. In 1940 he devoted a double page in the *Hamburger Illustrierte* to 'Nessie', exposing her as a cunning invention by British tourist agencies. A year later Mussolini's paper *Popolo d'Italia* printed the news that bombing of Britain had been so intense and successful that the Loch Ness Monster had been killed by a direct hit. An Italian bomber pilot had apparently claimed to have 'straddled Nessie with a stick of bombs and left her lying on the surface'.

The creatures were, in fact, very far from such an ignominious demise. Eleven sightings were reported in 1941, despite the absence of tourists. In April 1944 Engineer-Commander R. A. R. Meiklem, R.N., and his wife watched the humped back of one of the animals cross the loch in front of their house in Fort Augustus. Mrs Meiklem remarked: 'It gave one a rather uncanny feeling, although I was delighted at having had such an excellent view of it for several minutes.' Their account was reported in a news bulletin sent to prisoners-of-war in Europe.

In May of the following year, Lieutenant Colonel W. H. Lane, his wife and two neighbours watched a similar display from their home at Tigh-na-Bruach, just south of Invermoriston. One of them said 'It was a huge black object. Watching it closely, it remained about two minutes on the surface after which it suddenly disappeared leaving a big wake on the loch.' Colonel Lane, who studied the wake through binoculars, said 'There was a slight curve in the wake, which looked, as far as I can judge, as if a moving torpedo was in the water. There can be no doubt it was made by a large, fast-moving object.'

It is impossible to calculate the number of sightings made during the war. The areas to the west of the loch were all restricted and were used for military purposes. Soldiers were stationed around the loch but because of an embargo on reporting troop movements the press could not refer to any sightings by them. The loch itself was used for testing equipment. It is known that during the First World War two submarines passed through it. Whether or not they had any unusual encounters is not known. However, during the Second World War one vessel of Her Majesty's Royal Navy did, according to its commander, encounter one of the animals. It hit one.

In 1943 Francis Russell Flint was a Lieutenant Commander in charge of a motor launch on passage through the Caledonian Canal from Leith to Swansea. On board were twenty other officers and ratings. In 1969 Commander Russell Flint described what happened: 'It was a gorgeous sunny day. We were heading south from Inverness in the vicinity of Fort Augustus, travelling at our top speed of about twenty-five knots. We were taking things easy when there was the most terrific jolt. Everybody was knocked back. And then we looked for'ard. And there it was. There was a very large animal form which disappeared in a flurry of water. It was definitely a living creature – certainly not debris or anything like that.'

Commander Russell Flint immediately sent the following signal to the Admiralty: 'Regret to inform your Lordships, damage to starboard bow following collision with Loch Ness

Monster. Proceeding at reduced speed to Fort Augustus.' Apparently their Lordships were not much impressed by this signal, and Commander Russell Flint received 'a bit of a blast' when he returned to base.

This experience is unique in that it is the only claim to have made physical contact with one of the animals. The beast must have been either very drowsy (it was, as Commander Russell Flint states, 'a gorgeous sunny day') or perhaps unwell not to have been aware of the approaching launch. The animals usually seem hypersensitive to noise and dive immediately.

After the war, as life slowly returned to normal, visitors began to trickle back to the Highlands. A newspaper reported in August 1947: 'An attempt has been made to relaunch the Loch Ness Monster, fun-topic of 1933. Thirty people claimed they saw it yesterday – complete with two humps.'

'Nessie's' big newspaper splash in 1950 suggested that, despite Commander Russell Flint's claim, the Royal Navy was as scornful about the whole affair as the rest of the establishment. The *Daily Herald* of 8 November 1950 carried a provocative headline, 'The Secret of Loch Ness', under which it was stated that 'The Navy knows the real truth about the Loch Ness Monster ... hitherto the explanation has been a top secret known only to a few but now, after 32 years, the secrecy ban has been removed.'

Splendid sensationalist journalism – the *Daily Herald* must have sold well that day, as, no doubt, did newspapers all over the world which took up the story. Actually the shattering disclosure turned out to relate to a number of eight-foot diameter, four-horned uncharged mines that had been anchored in Loch Ness in August 1918, at depths of between '600 feet and one mile' (which is strange in itself since the greatest recorded depth is only just under 1,000 feet). According to the *Daily Herald* H.M.S. *Welbeck* had found the loch to be seven miles deep.

Admiralty experts, it was reported, had been having a quiet chuckle about the 'Monster' since 1933 but had never previously divulged that its true identity was in fact a string of naval mines. Scottish newspapers immediately rallied to the animals' defence. 'Highlands Ablaze in Defence of "Nessie"', reported the *Aberdeen Press and Journal*; ' "Nessie" Just Mines? Highlanders Howl', said the *Daily Record*; 'Daily Paper Successfully Spoofed', said the *Inverness Courier*. The truth was that in 1922 another vessel had been to Loch Ness and recovered all the mine anchors. The mines were not found, and since they were designed to have a life of only a few years they were obviously on the bottom. Hugh Gray, who fifteen years later was to photograph one of the animals, was on board H.M.S. *Welbeck* in 1918 when the mines were laid. He said: 'Some of the mines came to the surface shortly after they had been laid down but the terrific pressure had made them as flat as pancakes. From that day to this there is no record of anyone seeing a mine in the loch.'

The *Inverness Courier* remarked scornfully (10 November 1950) that the only thing which had gone bang was the *Daily Herald*'s story, which exploded in its own face!

The next development in the story came the following year, on 14 July 1951, when another good photograph of one of the animals was taken. The photographer was Mr Lachlan Stuart, a thirty-year-old local woodsman, and the place was Whitefield, a croft about 100 feet above the water on the south shore opposite Urquhart Bay. This is Mr Stuart's account of what happened:

I got up at about 6.30 a.m. to milk the cow. When I looked out of the window I saw what I took to be a boat speeding along the middle of the loch towards Dores.

But I decided it was going too fast for a boat. It looked like a hump. Then another hump appeared and I thought it must be the monster which has been seen several times in this vicinity this week.

I shouted to my wife Elsie and to Taylor Hay, who stays with us, to come. I grabbed my camera (a small box camera) and hurried down the hill. Taylor followed. [Scottish *Daily Express*, 15 July 1951]

When the two men got to the water's edge the animal had turned and was now heading south only about fifty yards off shore. Mr Stuart continued:

I focused my camera on it, saw the three humps in the viewfinder and snapped it.

75

The beast was making for a point which juts out into the loch about 40 yards away. The three humps were visible all the time and in front of them was a long thin neck and a head about the size and shape of a sheep's head. The head and neck kept bobbing down into the water.

After he had taken the picture the animal began to head for the shore, and Mr Stuart and Mr Hay backed away into the trees. Then it turned and made off towards the centre of the loch. 'When it was about 300 yards out it submerged, head first, then the three humps, one after the other. We watched the spot for five or ten minutes, but saw nothing more.'

Mr Hay said: 'As it passed us the monster was going at about ten m.p.h. We saw three humps quite plainly gliding along through the water, with the head and neck bobbing up and down – hunting fish, we thought.'

Constance Whyte, who was living in Inverness at the time, saw the negative and a copy of the photograph that afternoon. Three days later she visited Mr Stuart at his home and got to know him and his family. She wrote in *More Than a Legend*:

I could not put forward this photograph with more confidence if I had taken it myself ... In Mr Stuart's opinion each of the humps measured about five feet in length at the surface of the water with some eight feet of water between each. The first hump stood about two feet out of the water, the second four feet and the third three feet. The neck and head together would be about six feet long. There was commotion in the water for 15 to 20 feet behind the last hump indicating, he thought, a tail moving. The skin he found difficult to describe; he could only say that it was not hairy and appeared uniform in colour, blackish. Some days later examining the photograph with Mr Stuart I asked him specifically about various points. He repeated that the head was like that of a sheep but without ears and horns, and about a foot long. He did not notice any eyes. The neck thickened suddenly to join the first hump. I asked him if the angular appearance of the humps was some kind of photographic illusion, but he thought not; his impression was that the humps did indeed look somewhat angular. Mr Stuart thought too from its movements and ability to manoeuvre in comparatively shallow water that the creature must be propelled by limbs as well as a powerful tail.

After he had taken the picture Mr Stuart had intended finishing off the film before getting it developed. But news of the morning's event had reached the Scottish *Daily Express* correspondent in Inverness via Mr Stuart's employer, and he met Mr Stuart as he returned home from work at lunchtime. The film was removed from the camera and taken to Mr John MacPherson, a commercial photographer in Cawdor, who developed it. He said: 'The film appeared to be perfectly normal in every way. Mr Stuart said he took the snap at 6.30 a.m. and the picture was dull enough to have been taken at that time.'

The photograph made some temporary impact. There was a new surge of interest, and Mr C. Eric Palmar, Curator of Natural History at a Glasgow museum, was sufficiently inspired by it to make what can only be described as a brave comment:

The representation in the picture could possibly be three abnormal-sized seals chasing and playing with each other, but this seems unlikely. A feasible explanation is that the 'Monster' may be some type of deep water animal which only rarely comes to the surface. It is possible that these animals were cut off in Loch Ness from the ocean many ages ago by earth movements and their descendants have managed to survive.

As a result of the new publicity the BBC decided it was time for them to make some contribution to the investigation, and preparations were begun for a special television inquiry. A ninety-minute programme was broadcast on 26 September 1951 and consisted of a courtroom trial of the 'Monster', with a counsel for fact, Mr 'Verity', and a counsel for legend advocating before a judge and jury. The entire script had been prepared beforehand, and although a number of eye-witnesses, including Alex Campbell, Lady Maud Baillie and Mr Lachlan Stuart, made personal appearances, there was little attempt at an objective survey of the evidence. A critic in *The Listener* (11 October 1951) wrote: 'Rarely has so compelling a subject for the viewing majority been more fantastically maltreated.' The programme had included, for some reason, a survey of cattle ranching in Scotland and a parody of press activities at the loch in 1933.

The latter portrayed 'Denis Walters', a Fleet Street journalist, and 'Bill Briggs' his photographer, evidently at their wits' end to produce a story. Walters complains: 'Nobody's seen the monster for five days. I gave a kid ten bob today, but he wouldn't say he'd seen the damned thing. His mother gave me the money back. She said I was corrupting her bairn and she'd get the polis if I did it again.' So they build a model out of barrels and motor tyres which they plan to haul across the loch surface by an ingenious system of ropes, pulleys and drainpipes which lead up through the kitchen sink of a conveniently situated ruined croft. Their dastardly scheme is foiled by 'Donald the Deer-stalker', who steals the model and hurries off to the pub, where he finds 'Dunfield', another reporter, brandishing a stuffed hippopotamus hoof which he has been stamping all over the neighbourhood. The sequence closed with a newspaper headline flashed across the screen: 'Loch Ness Sensation. Monster has Four Left Feet.'

The last witness called on the programme was Dr Maurice Burton, at the time a Deputy Keeper of Zoology at the British Museum of Natural History, who told the 'court' that although most of his colleagues did not believe in the animals, he had an open mind. As we shall see, Dr Burton's mind was later to oscillate from being one of the phenomenon's staunchest zoological supporters to being its arch-critic. The final verdict of the programme was 'Not Proven'. To quote *The Listener*'s critic again: 'Writing about the Loch Ness Monster enquiry requires a restraint that is as hard to bear as the programme, television's biggest let-down for some time.'

However, 1951 produced several good sightings in addition to Lachlan Stuart's. The following is an account by Mr J. Harper-Smith, O.B.E., Ll.B., Town Clerk of Lincoln. During June 1951 he spent several days in Inverness-shire on a fishing holiday with his son, an Army officer.

We went over to the village of Dores to inquire about hiring a boat. After arranging this we had a chat with the old lady who runs the Dores Inn. I asked her if the locals believed in the 'Monster'. She looked at me very seriously and said: 'It isn't a question of believing in it – most of us have seen it at one time or another and we *know* it is there.' Unfortunately (for me) I still remained sceptical.

The next afternoon we went out fishing but because it was wet when we set out I left my cine camera and binoculars behind. By about 9 p.m. the loch was like a mirror. We were just starting to take down our rods when my son pointed with his arm and said: 'Is that a periscope over there?'

I looked and realized something was coming up out of the water. Within a few seconds a black head was followed by a similar-coloured neck several feet long. While we were eagerly looking for the body the head and neck began moving forward at a very fast speed followed by a huge wash. As it came nearer we noticed some oscillations of the head and neck. We began to edge in nearer the shore but when it had come to within about 800 yards 'it' turned and went back up the centre of the loch and shortly afterwards submerged. We put the length of the neck at about five feet and the diameter at about a foot . . .

Mr Harper-Smith concluded by saying: 'I live in hope that I may one day be fortunate enough to recapture what was the greatest thrill of my life.'

At about midday on 13 November 1951 Colonel Patrick Grant, at that time owner of Knockie Lodge, high up in the hills behind the 'Horseshoe' shore line, was driving north out of Fort Augustus.

Quite suddenly I noticed a great disturbance in the water at about 150 yards from the shore . . . I saw a length, perhaps six feet, of some black object showing a foot or less out of the water and as I looked the object disappeared and reappeared a moment later at least a hundred yards away and nearer the shore. The speed of movement was very great. I am positive that what I saw was a living creature but not a porpoise or a whale or a big seal. [*Inverness Courier*, 16 November 1951]

Unknown to Colonel Grant this sighting was also witnessed by Mrs A. C. Kirton, wife of a Fort Augustus doctor, from a wooden bridge over the River Oich. She independently corroborated the disturbance and the appearance of the hump at the time and place reported by the Colonel.

In 1952 tragedy struck Loch Ness when it took the life of

John Cobb as he became the fastest man to travel on water. With his 6,000 h.p. £15,000 speedboat *Crusader* he arrived at the loch on 26 August to try to add the world water speed record to the land speed record which he already held. Late on the morning of 29 September, he made one northerly run up the mirror-calm surface of the loch. Then he turned and commenced the run which was to take him to a record-breaking speed of 206 m.p.h. along the specially marked-out mile and which ended in the disintegration of *Crusader* and his death. The accident happened when *Crusader* hit a patch of turbulence. Inevitably there have been suggestions that the animals caused the small disturbance which threw the boat into such violent vibration that it literally fell apart. However, it is now accepted that the ripples were the remnants of the reflected wake from the first run slowly settling on the surface.

John Cobb was recovered alive from the wreckage, wearing a special inflatable suit, and he was carried up the hill to Achnahannet where he died. A stone memorial now stands at the roadside, erected in memory of 'A very gallant Gentleman' by the people of Glen Urquhart.

*

During recent years the underwater radar mechanism known as sonar has played an invaluable part in the research at Loch Ness. The first indication of the potential of this sort of equipment as a 'monster-hunting' tool came in December 1954, when a drifter picked up a strange outline on its echo-sounding apparatus.

At about 11.30 a.m. on 2 December the Peterhead drifter *Rival III* was approaching Urquhart Castle on its journey south through the Caledonian Canal to the West Coast fishing grounds. In the wheelhouse was the forty-six-year-old mate, Mr Peter Anderson. The skipper, Mr Donald MacLean, and the seven other crew members were below having a cup of tea. Mr Anderson glanced at the echo sounder, a Kelvin Hughes 'Fishmaster', and stiffened.

Suddenly the printer arm on the machine started to draw this thing on the roll of recording paper.

As it sketched it out I couldn't believe my eyes. For several minutes the arm went on moving and the outlines of the thing below the water were drawn on the paper. I shouted to the crew and they came crowding up to the wheelhouse. They were as amazed as I was. At once we turned the boat about and tried to track the 'Monster' again. But it was no use, whatever it was had gone. [*Daily Herald*, 6 December 1954]

Mr Anderson tore the chart from the machine, and as the boat passed through the locks down to the West Coast he brought it out and showed it to the Canal staff. By the time the *Rival III* reached Oban the press was waiting for them and negotiations began for the exclusive rights to the chart. The *Daily Herald* eventually won, and while on 5 December the *Sunday Mail* reported rather sourly that the chart 'is not for sale', representatives of the manufacturers of the equipment were examining it under the auspices of the *Herald*.

Mr L. A. Southcott, the firm's District Manager, and Mr A. Sutton, the Technical Development Director, both examined the chart and certified that it had not been faked or tampered with in any way. From the calibrated scale they could tell that the object was 480 feet deep and 120 feet up from the loch bed. It was moving from left to right on the chart, that is, in the same direction as the boat, and was approximately fifty feet in length. Mr Sutton stated, after a long study of the graph: 'It is definitely not a water-logged tree or a shoal of fish. These give entirely different signals. If there was a large animal in the loch this is the kind of image you would get from an echo sounder ... I can't explain it away. I have seen thousands of recordings – but nothing like this.'

Mr Southcott said: 'This is definitely animal matter of some kind ... in all my experience I've never seen anything like this. The object certainly is not like any other kind of fish that has been charted.' All that could be said about the shape of the object was that it was elongated and probably irregular.

Among the people consulted by the press for an opinion on the chart was Dr C. H. Mortimer of the Freshwater Biological Association, who had carried out a temperature survey at the loch in 1953. He was quoted in the *Daily Herald* of 7 December as saying: 'I too got some unusual recordings on Loch Ness. I explained them away to my own satisfaction then as echoes from the side of the loch superimposing themselves on the sounding chart. But from the graph description the object appears to be clear of the sides of the loch. It is extremely puzzling.'

One person feeling more frustrated than puzzled by the event was the wife of the *Rival III*'s skipper, Mrs Betty MacLean. She was quoted as saying: 'I am the laughing stock of Peterhead. Everyone looks at me and smiles. While I was out shopping, fishermen and their wives were looking at me as if I had got the "Monster" in my shopping bag.'

Unfortunately, whatever serious interest was reawakened was marred by yet another hoax. On 8 December a Royal Naval mine-laying vessel reported to Canal staff that they too had picked up a strange echo whilst on passage through the loch. As soon as the press arrived the commander admitted that it was all a joke, and the cursing reporters left to vent their anger at the whole matter.

In April 1957 Constance Whyte's book *More Than a Legend* was published (by Hamish Hamilton). It was the first attempt in the twenty-three years since the publication of Commander Gould's book to collate the evidence and present the 'Monster' as a serious subject worthy of scientific study. Mrs Whyte, a qualified doctor married to the Manager and Engineer of the Caledonian Canal, Frank Whyte, had moved to Inverness in 1937. Twelve years later she was asked to write an article on the 'Monster' for a privately circulated magazine, and what till then had been a casual interest in the mystery was changed to a fascination as she delved more deeply into the mine of reported information. Describing the reasons for writing the book Mrs Whyte, who never saw the animals herself despite living in Inverness for twenty-three years, writes:

A book had to be written. The search for truth is always worth-while but in this instance it was the vindication of many people of integrity who had reported honestly what they had seen in Loch Ness which was my main motive. Friends of mine had been subjected to ridicule and contempt and I felt it was time to counteract the flippant and frivolous attitude of the Press and of the media generally.

The success of *More Than A Legend* was reflected in the volume of correspondence received by the author. Its publication was undoubtedly the first and very significant turning-point towards the modern campaign of serious investigation.

When the book was first published, Crompton Library Committee in Lancashire was one of several which refused to stock it. 'The Loch Ness Monster is a lot of tomfoolery,' said Councillor F. H. Sykes of Crompton. However, after the Chairman had actually read the book they changed their minds.

It was perhaps a wise decision, since interest in the 'Monster' was undoubtedly increasing as more and more people visited the Highlands every year. As an example let us take a very ordinary sighting and see the extent to which it was publicized throughout the world. On 11 March 1957 Inspector John Grant of Inverness-shire police, Mr Derek Fowles, a teacher at Fort Augustus Abbey School, and Mr Ian Grant, a garage proprietor, all watched a two-humped object moving in the loch near Drumnadrochit. Thanks to the zeal and efficiency of the international press agencies, this story appeared in literally hundreds of newspapers all over the world. The *New York Post* headlined it 'A Sure Sign of Spring – The Loch Ness Monster'; the *Irish Press* wrote about its being 'the sure sign of the start of the silly season.' Elsewhere, the sighting was reported in, to name but a few, the *Mid-Ocean News*, Bermuda; the *Diamond Fields Advertisers*, Kimberley in Australia; the *Iraq Times*, Baghdad; the *Buenos Aires Herald*; and the *Otago Daily Times* of New Zealand.

In view of this worldwide interest it seems quite proper that on 15 March a toast to 'Nessie's' health was proposed in the House of Commons by Mr John Rankin, Labour, during a debate on industry in the North of Scotland.

Two months later Mr Hector Hughes, another Labour M.P., got up in the House and asked the Secretary of State for Scotland, Mr John Maclay, whether he would be prepared to authorize the use of the latest underwater viewing and listening devices to locate the animals. Referring to *More Than a Legend*

Mr Hughes said: 'Does not the Secretary of State realize that he owes an obligation to science in this matter and that recent learned works have indicated that such a survey might reveal the existence in Loch Ness of a prehistoric or unique monster, fish or reptile, of some kind, the discovery of which might add considerably to science?' The Secretary of State refused, and the debate closed with a suggestion by another member that Mr Hughes should literally 'go and jump into the lake' and look for the 'Monster' himself.

This debate prompted the *Washington Star* to write a leading article deploring any such attempt at finding the animals. 'The Loch Ness Monster', it wrote, 'is one of the world's nicest and most engaging personalities ... Leave him alone. Hands off. Mind your own business, Mr Hughes.'

A very spirited display by one of the animals was put up in December of 1957. Mr Raymond Bain, a Fort Augustus resident, was driving north along the lochside about three miles south of Urquhart Castle when his attention was attracted by the appearance of a large animal swimming swiftly in the loch about 150 yards out. He saw a long neck and head, swan-like in outline, and a thirty-foot-long black body. However, the most impressive thing about the animal was its speed. 'I paced the beast with my car,' he said ,'but I could not keep up with it although I was travelling at 35 m.p.h. Sometimes it would slow down and I would catch up with it and then it would dash off again.' The animal eventually disappeared near Urquhart Castle. Mr Bain added 'Now there is no doubt in my mind that the loch holds a very strange, large, extraordinarily powerful animal.'

By the spring of 1958 several expeditions were in the planning stage. A team of fifty Scottish divers announced that they were to plumb the loch's depths, and Mr H. L. Cockrell, a fish hatchery owner from Dumfries, said that he was going to set out in an Eskimo kayak to look for the animals, armed with a camera and a commando knife. This news prompted Mr Hector Hughes into yet more Parliamentary activity. He tabled a question asking what action the Scottish Secretary proposed to take to protect 'this valuable Scottish asset'. He also reiterated his earlier demand for a Government-equipped expedition. His call was, predictably, ignored in Parliamentary circles.*

However, the Royal Navy was being linked with a new BBC programme on the phenomenon. In March the press got to hear about a scheme whereby the Navy would, as a training exercise, provide a vessel equipped with ASDIC and echo sounders to be used by the BBC to carry out sweeps of the loch. The leader columns immediately waxed indignant and the Admiralty had second thoughts and withdrew their support.

Nevertheless, the BBC persevered and *The Legend of the Loch* was broadcast to an audience of about eight million people on 15 May, just twenty-five years after it had all begun. It was an outside broadcast direct from the loch and involved producer John Buchan and his technical team of fifty engineers in the most complex transmission ever attempted till then. Judging from the massive press build-up and the subsequent reviews, it was a great success.

Commentator Raymond Baxter interviewed a number of eye-witnesses, including J. Harper Smith and Dr Richard Synge. A team of frogmen was shown operating underwater television cameras off Urquhart Castle, which admirably demonstrated the problems of working underwater in the gloom of Loch Ness. Although naturally there was no timely surface appearance by one of the animals to make the programme complete, one of them apparently had a tantalizingly brief encounter with the BBC's echo-sounding equipment about an hour before the programme went on the air.

The BBC's boat, the Clyde puffer *Kaffir*, was crossing Urquhart Bay, having picked up the engineering crew to take up station off the Castle. Mr David Anderson, operator of the Marconi echo sounder aboard *Kaffir*, explained what happened: 'The object was picked up seventy yards north-east of Urquhart Castle. I cut the sensitivity back and the object re-

* So too was a speech he made in Parliament in May about a giant alligator-like claw which a Loch Ness resident claimed to have found on the shore. Mr Hughes asked the question of Parliament: 'Do you not think it is stultifying in this scientific age not to take serious notice of the important discoveries which may be made there?'

appeared – as a black heavy mark. I pointed it out to Mr Baxter. The object was fairly large, maybe twenty feet long, and diving away from the vessel at between three and ten fathoms, causing considerable agitation of the water.'

Whatever it was, its echo was quite unlike that of either a single fish or a shoal. None of the Marconi technicians could suggest what it was. It had dived from a depth of twelve feet to sixty feet before it was lost.

The BBC was not the only organization in the film world anxious to make a star out of 'Nessie'. The British film industry decided in 1958 that it was time they produced their answer to Hollywood's monster from 20,000 fathoms, and the obvious candidate for such a part was 'Nessie'. The result was *The Giant Behemoth,* in which the 'Monster' turns out to be a prehistoric radio-active palaeosaurus over 200 feet long which abandons its tedious life in the Highlands, travels south and runs amuck in London, trampling over various famous landmarks.

The year also produced two still photographs. One of them was taken by Mr H. L. Cockrell, whose canoeing plans caused the Parliamentary question earlier in the year. During the late summer he spent several days at the loch paddling about its enigmatic waters with a specially rigged flash camera attached to his life-jacket. On his final night-operation he encountered something moving in the water which may have been one of the animals – or, as Mr Cockrell says, it may have been just a stick. This is his story as printed in the *Weekly Scotsman* (16 October 1958):

Just about dawn I had my first real test. A light breeze suddenly dropped and left me on a mirror surface about halfway between shores with Invermoriston almost abeam to starboard. Something appeared – or I noticed it for the first time – about 50 yards away on my port bow. It seemed to be swimming very steadily and converging on me. It looked like a very large flat head four or five feet long and wide. About three feet astern of this I noticed another thin line. All very low in the water just awash.

I was convinced it was the head and neck of a very large creature ... I simply could not believe it. I was not a bit amused. With a considerable effort of will I swung in to intercept and to my horror it appeared to sheer towards me with ponderous power.

I hesitated. There was no-one anywhere near on that great sheet of water to witness a retreat but it was obviously too late to run. Curiously enough I found this a great relief. My heart began to beat normally and my muscles suddenly felt in good trim. I took a shot with my camera in case I got too close for my focus and went in ...
There was a light squall out of the glen behind Invermoriston and the object appeared to sink. When the squall cleared I could still see something on the surface. I closed in again cautiously. It remained motionless and I found it was a long stick about an inch thick.

I arrived home and really believed my particular 'Monster' was a stick until the films were developed.

The film showed quite a large affair which had a distinct wash. There was no reason for this wash as the picture also shows the water mirror calm ... What caused the wash? Could it have been 'Nessie' after all? I just don't know.

A week after Mr Cockrell's story and picture appeared in the *Weekly Scotsman* the paper published another photograph, which had been sent in by an interested reader, Mr P. A. Macnab, a bank manager and County Councillor in Ayrshire. Mr Macnab had taken his photograph on the early afternoon of Friday 29 July 1955, but 'through diffidence and fear of ridicule I have kept it to myself until now.' His photograph, which has since joined the Surgeon's and Lachlan Stuart's to become a Loch Ness classic, shows a long dark object of considerable size off Urquhart Castle tower. Here, for the first time, is the complete story of how he took it and one other photograph which he shortly afterwards destroyed:

I was returning from a holiday in the north with my son and pulled the car up on the road just above Urquhart Castle. It was a calm, warm hazy afternoon. I was all ready to take a shot of Urquhart Castle when my attention was held by a movement in the calm water over to the left. Naturally I thought of the 'Monster' and hurriedly changed over the standard lens of my Exacta (127) camera to a six-inch telephoto. As I was doing so a quick glance showed that some black or dark enormous water creature was cruising on the surface.

Without a tripod and in a great hurry I took the shot. I also took a very quick shot with another camera, a fixed-focus Kodak, before the creature submerged.

My son was busy under the bonnet of the car at the time and when he looked in response to my shouts there were just ripples on the water. Several cars and a bus stopped but they could see nothing and listened to my description with patent disbelief.

Disbelief is what Mr Macnab also found after he had developed the photographs and shown them to friends. 'So great was the scepticism and the leg-pulling by friends to whom I showed the picture that in a spirit of exasperation I threw the second negative away and nearly got rid of the first as well.'

The animal was travelling from left to right at about eight knots. The photograph has an added importance because size and scale can be deduced from the Castle tower in the corner, which is sixty-four feet high. Mr Macnab himself says he thinks there may be two creatures visible in the photograph, but even so the one hump is extremely large and would appear to be in the region of fifty feet in length.

*

And so we come to the end of twenty years of 'Monster' history. 1959 saw interest reviving even more. An Italian journalist claimed he had invented 'Nessie' back in 1933 when he had been short of a story one week; 'Beppo', a famous circus clown, went for a dive in the loch and was dragged out delirious, mumbling about 'unseen eyes' looking at him from slimy black depths; the 'Monster' was the subject of a sketch at the Edinburgh Festival; in November the fishing vessel *Guiding Star* picked up yet another inexplicable echo sounding of an object moving in the water column; and a diver from Hong Kong remarked after a fruitless search: 'I look hard down there, but I no see her!'

The phenomenon was about to be subjected to the period of most intense investigation in its history. However, before studying the excitement and achievements of the Loch Ness investigation we shall first look at what is perhaps the most remarkable feature of the whole Loch Ness story: the strange habit which the animals apparently have of leaving the loch and coming ashore.

Chapter Six

The Monster Comes Ashore

Many visitors to Loch Ness arrive half expecting to see its 'Monster' gambolling playfully in the water. Very few realize that they could meet one of the animals on land. Evidence suggests that very occasionally these strange creatures leave their natural environment and heave their massive bulks ashore, thus becoming, it would seem, the largest land animals in the world.

For the earliest traceable land sightings we go back to the time of the First World War and join a teenage Fort Augustus girl playing on the shingly beach at Inchnacardoch Bay. The late Mrs Margaret Cameron was the young girl in question, and when I had the pleasure of meeting her in the summer of 1971 she described what happened late one warm Sunday afternoon in the month of September:

I was with my two brothers and my young sister Lizzie, who was in the pram. We were waiting for some friends and were passing the time by skimming stones across the water when we heard this awful crackling in the trees on the other side of the little bay.

It must have been something awfully big, we thought; and of course we had been warned not to go near the loch by our grandparents, as there were these wild horses in the loch, and we thought now this must be one of them!

So we sat for a wee while and this crackling seemed to be coming nearer and nearer, and then, suddenly, this big thing appeared out of the trees and started to move down the beach to the water. I couldn't tell you if it had a long neck or a short neck because it was pointing straight at us. It had a huge body and its movement as it came out of the trees was like a caterpillar. I would say it was a good twenty feet long – what we saw of it. Now, the colour of it – I

89

hadn't seen an elephant in them days, but it's the colour of the elephant, and it seemed to have rather a shiny skin. Under it we saw two short, round feet at the front and it lurched to one side and put one foot into the water and then the other one. We didn't wait to see the end of it coming out – we got too big a fright. When we got home we were all sick and couldn't take our tea. So we had to explain what had happened and we told our mum and dad, and grandfather was there and I can see him banging the table and telling us not to tell anybody about it. Anyway, we were put to bed with a big dose of castor oil ... . It's still so very vivid in my mind – I'll never forget it.

Inchnacardoch Bay is about 150 yards wide, and although the children had only a comparatively short look at the animal emerging from the trees and bushes it was enough to tell them that it was quite unlike any other creature they had ever seen.

In contrast to the tranquillity of the setting of Mrs Cameron's experience, the next land sighting took place on a wet, blustery night in February 1919. The witnesses on this occasion were Mr Jock Forbes, then a boy of twelve, and his father, a farmer in Foyers. They were returning late one night from the cattle sales in Inverness in their pony cart. Like Mrs Cameron's sighting above, the following details, as described to fellow-researcher Alan Jones and myself by Jock Forbes, have not been published before:

It was a very dark, stormy night. My father and I had stopped off at my uncle's house at Scaniport and then continued on our journey. We were about two miles north of Inverfarigaig near the old ferry, where the bank isn't very steep, when the pony suddenly stopped and started backing away in fright. It very nearly backed us right off the road and down the bank.

Something large was crossing the road about twenty yards ahead of us – it came out of the trees above the road, moved slowly across the road and then down the bank and we heard a splash as, presumably, it went into the water.

It was too dark and I was too busy trying to control the pony to notice any details, but it was certainly a big beast, fully the width of the road.

My father, I remember, muttered something in Gaelic and after a moment or two we hurried on home and never really mentioned it again.

We asked Mr Forbes whether, as a boy, he had ever heard any stories of unusual animals having been seen on land. He replied that it was quite well known that a tinker lady at about the turn of the century had once come across a strange creature lying beside the Dores to Foyers road. The experience apparently so terrified her that henceforth she always made a long detour over the hills to avoid the spot.

Although both of these accounts refer to a large animal on land, neither really contains sufficient detail for us to be able to identify the animal with those seen in the water. Mrs Cameron could not see a neck but she did see two 'short, round feet' which, at the distance from which she was viewing, could have been flippers being used as legs in a seal-like manner. The next account confuses matters even more since the description is, in some respects, at variance with the image of the animals we can build up from the majority of eye-witness reports.

At about 5 a.m. on an April morning in 1923, Mr Alfred Cruickshank was driving his Model T Ford along the very hazardous road which preceded the A82 along the loch's northern shore. He was a chauffeur on his way from his home in Buckie to meet his employer on the train from Glasgow arriving at Speanbridge at 8 a.m. It was still dark, and Mr Cruickshank's route was being illuminated by the car's rather primitive headlamps as he bumped and wound his way along the deserted road. About two miles north of Invermoriston he crested a small hill and his headlamps picked out a large object on the outside of a bend in the road about fifty yards ahead of him.

I could see something moving – it had a large humped body standing about six feet high with its belly trailing on the ground and about twelve feet long, to which was attached a long thick tail which was ten to twelve feet in length. It was moving slowly, sort of waddling away from the road on two legs which I could see on the near side.

I saw the outline of what appeared to be the head, which was big and pug-nosed and was set right on the body – in other words it didn't seem to have much of a neck.

I was slowing down to go round the corner so the lamps faded, but as I went round the corner I heard a grunting noise from where it was. I stopped the car once I was round the corner, but I couldn't turn the car round and I certainly wasn't going back on foot.

Mr Cruickshank described the colour as dark olive to khaki and lighter underneath, although obviously in the poor light it was difficult to determine colour clearly. The most discordant detail in Mr Cruickshank's story is the absence of the characteristic long, slender neck. When asked whether it was possible that the head was turned in his direction, thus giving the impression of a large head and no neck, he told me that he did not think this was so, neither did he feel that the head and neck could have been shielded from his view by bushes.

The most important consideration is that Mr Cruickshank is quite adamant that he saw a twenty- to twenty-five-foot-long animal moving by the side of the road. The fact that some of the details are inconsistent with our usual picture of the animals is perhaps understandable in view of the poor light and the brevity of his sighting. Such inconsistencies show, as has already been pointed out, that an individual witness is describing what he saw and is not adjusting his account to fall into line with others.

When Mr Cruickshank arrived at Speanbridge station and met his employer, the latter apparently asked him what was wrong, since he was looking very pale. 'He thought I must have had an accident,' recalled Mr Cruickshank, 'but I told him what had happened, and he said I must have been dreaming. A couple of other friends whom I told about the sighting said I must have been drunk. Apart from them I just told my wife and then kept quiet about it all.' Mr Cruickshank also recalled that towards the end of the 1920s he spoke to a girl working in a baker's shop in Fort Augustus who told him that she had once seen a large animal hauled up on to a beach near Fort Augustus. 'She said that she was coming down the hill east of the village on her bicycle when she saw a big animal lying on the beach below her. She was so frightened she jumped off her bicycle and ran the rest of the way home.'

The most famous land sighting of all is, of course, that witnessed by Mr and Mrs F. T. G. Spicer on 22 July 1933. George Spicer was a director of a firm of central London tailors, Messrs Todhouse, Reynard and Company. On the day in question they were returning home from a holiday in the North of Scotland. Before we proceed with their story it should be remembered that in July 1933 the 'Monster' was still a subject of relative obscurity; neither Mr nor Mrs Spicer had any idea that Loch Ness was supposed to harbour strange animals, which made their encounter with one even more stunning for them.

It was about 4 o'clock on a quiet summer afternoon. George Spicer was driving his Austin car south along the undulating Dores to Foyers road. They were about midway between the two villages and travelling at about twenty m.p.h. Suddenly Mrs Spicer exclaimed: 'What on earth is that?'

About 200 yards ahead of them a horizontal trunk-like object was emerging from the bushes above the road. It was undulating into two or three arches and was held several feet above the road surface. Mr Spicer later likened it to a 'scenic railway'. The trunk was rapidly followed by a ponderous body. Mr Spicer takes up the story:*

It was horrible – an abomination. It did not move in the usual reptilian fashion but with these arches. The body shot across the road in jerks but because of the slope we could not see its lower parts and saw no limbs.

Although I accelerated towards it, it had vanished by the time we reached the spot. I got out of the car and could see where it had gone down through the bracken, but there was no sign of it in the water. The body was about five feet in height and filled the road. If it had stopped I should have done likewise as there was no room to turn the car round and it was quite big enough to have upset our car.

I estimated the length to be twenty-five to thirty feet. Its colour so far as the body is concerned could only be called a dark elephant grey. We saw no tail, nor did I notice any mouth on what I took to be the head of the creature. We later concluded that the tail must have been curled around alongside it since there was something protruding above its shoulder which gave the impression that it was carrying something on its back. My wife and I looked at each other in amazement. It had been a loathsome sight. To see that arched neck straggle across was something which still haunts us.

*This account is put together from letters from Mr Spicer and press accounts at the time.

The Spicers continued on their way and met a cyclist. This was William McCulloch, a native of Foyers, who when he heard their story was, according to Mr Spicer, 'astounded – not frightened, just incredulous. He added that he was glad we had seen it because people were laughing at a bus-driver friend of his in the village who had reported seeing it.' After the Spicers had driven on, Mr McCulloch cycled to the spot where they told him the animal had crossed, and he gave (previously unpublished) confirmation that the undergrowth was flattened, both above the road and below it down to the lochside. 'It was as if a steamroller had been through,' he said. When the Spicers reached Foyers Mr Spicer told several people what had happened but was either ignored or laughed at.

Although Mr Spicer wrote to the *Inverness Courier* in August, and the paper published his report, it was ignored until December, when the matter was given widespread coverage. In his letter to the *Courier* Mr Spicer appealed for information about this 'nearest approach to a dragon or pre-historic animal that I have ever seen in my life ...'; from the tone of his letter it is clear he was totally unaware of the 'Loch Ness Monster'. He continued: 'Whatever it is and it may be a land and water animal, I think it should be destroyed as I am not sure whether had I been close to it I should have cared to have tackled it.'

On 7 December the Spicers' story appeared in the *Daily Sketch* and they at once found themselves besieged by reporters. The account was inevitably distorted, and the object seen at the animal's shoulder was interpreted as being 'a lamb in its mouth.' Mr Spicer stated that he was 'willing to take an oath and make an affidavit and so is my wife, that we saw this beast.' A few days later he described the sighting on the famous BBC radio programme *In Town Tonight*. He wrote (in a letter to F. W. Holiday dated 16 December 1936): 'I have been ridiculed a good bit but I believe most people think there is something there now, as it has been seen many times in the loch.'

Commander Rupert Gould visited the Spicers and recorded this observation: 'I became and remain convinced that their story was entirely bona fide; that they had undergone a most

unusual experience which had left a lasting and rather unpleasant impression.'

Captain James Fraser, the leader of Sir Edward Mountain's
expedition, also met George Spicer when the latter revisited the
loch in 1934. He told me: 'I remember a man coming up to me
and asking me how things were going. We talked for a few
moments and then he told me who he was. He seemed a very
quiet, retiring man and was only just recovering from the ter-
rible ordeal of ridicule he and his wife had been through.'

In addition to the Spicer land sighting of 1933, one of the
animals was also evidently seen on land in August by Mrs M. F.
MacLennan of Drumnadrochit. She was walking along the
road south of Dores when she saw a strange creature lying on
the beach. She shouted to her husband, who was a short distance behind her, and the animal immediately plunged into the
water. Mrs MacLennan described it as a dark grey mass about
twenty to twenty-five feet long. She got an impression of a long
neck twisted round towards its back, a humped body and four
legs.

Mrs Reid, the wife of the postmaster at Inverfarigaig,
claimed at Christmas 1933 that she was travelling along the
road to Inverness when she saw an odd-looking animal lying in
the bracken. It was only about ten feet in length and dark in
colour. A Mr William MacLean of Inverness claimed that he
disturbed a large creature resting on the gravelly beach half a
mile west of Dores. Apparently it slithered off into the loch and
left a big wash. There is also a story that schoolchildren in
Drumnadrochit told their schoolmaster, some time in the early
1930s, that they had seen a most peculiar and horrifying animal
in the overgrown marsh area at the delta of the rivers flowing
into Urquhart Bay. Although it has not been possible to discover any further details of this last story, it is interesting because local legend states that, years ago, the animals quite often
used to crawl up the beds of the rivers flowing into Urquhart
Bay.

*

The land sighting of January 1934 has already been mentioned in connection with the activities of that pair of big-game hunters, Messrs Wetherall and Pauli. The details of the sighting, which comes a close second to the Spicers' in terms of notoriety, are as follows.

Mr W. Arthur Grant, a twenty-one-year-old veterinary student from Polmaily House, Glen Urquhart, was returning home from Inverness on his motorcycle at about 1 a.m. on Friday 5 January. Mr 'Bobo' Mackay, Provost of Inverness, a life-long and at times extremely vociferous sceptic, confirms that Mr Grant was perfectly sober when he left Inverness at about 12.30 a.m. after making some final adjustments to his motorcycle. The night was brightly moonlit and as Mr Grant approached the Abriachan turn he noticed, some forty yards ahead of him, a dark object in the shadow of the bushes on the opposite side of the road.

I was almost on it when it turned what I thought was a small head on a long neck in my direction. The creature apparently took fright and made two great bounds across the road and then went faster down to the loch, which it entered with a huge splash.

I jumped off my cycle and followed it but from the disturbance on the surface it had evidently made away before I reached the shore. I had a splendid view of the object. In fact, I almost struck it with my motorcycle. The body was very hefty. I distinctly saw two front flippers and there seemed to be two other flippers which were behind and which it used to spring from.

The tail would be from five to six feet long and very powerful; the curious thing about it was that the end was rounded off – it did not come to a point. The total length of the animal would be fifteen to twenty feet.

Mr Grant made a careful inspection of the path the animal had taken, marked the spot and went on home. When he arrived he woke his younger brother, told him what had happened and drew a sketch of what he had seen. Artist Alan Jones's reconstruction of the scene, reproduced here, is based on Mr Grant's original sketches and on photographs of the stretch of road where the beast crossed.

When it was light Mr Grant returned to the scene with

members of his family and they carried out another search for tracks or other remnants. None were found. The *Daily Mail* expedition (see Chapter 3) was then informed, and soon after they arrived, Messrs Wetherall and Pauli managed, as we have seen, to locate a pile of bones, a dead goat and some toe marks. It should be remembered that this was all happening the day after the Natural History Museum had identified Mr Wetherall's mysterious hoof-prints found near Dores as belonging to a hippopotamus. People were therefore in no mood to swallow a story of a land sighting, particularly after it had been dressed up with details of a half-eaten meal left at the roadside. Mr Grant found himself subjected to such violent ridicule that he was persuaded to tell some people that he had never seen the animal. The pressure on him became so unbearable that he had to miss a term at college.

The police took a special account of his experience, and Mr Grant made a statement to the Veterinary Society in Edinburgh. As a veterinary student he was, of course, in a rather better position than most as an observer. He said in a statement: 'Knowing something of natural history I can say that I have never seen anything in my life like the animal I saw. It looked like a hybrid ... It had a head rather like a snake or an eel, flat at the top, with a large oval eye, longish neck and somewhat longer tail. The body was much thicker towards the tail than was the front portion. In colour it was black or dark brown and had a skin rather like that of a whale. The head must have been about six feet from the ground as it crossed the road.'

From a major highway we move to a deserted beach for the next land sighting. At about 6.30 on the Sunday morning of 3 June 1934, a young housemaid, Miss Margaret Munro, looked out of a window at her employer's house, Kilchumein Lodge, which is set about 300 yards back from Borlum Bay, just east of Fort Augustus. She saw 'the largest living creature I have ever seen.' For the next twenty-five minutes she watched and studied through a pair of binoculars a large animal rolling on the shingly beach in the bright morning sunshine.

Most of the animal was clear of the water. It had 'a giraffe-like neck and an absurdly small head out of all proportion to the size of the body which was dark grey in colour. The under part of the chest was white and the skin was like an elephant's. Two very short forelegs or flippers were clearly seen. The animal kept turning itself in the sunshine, and it was able to arch its back into large humps. Finally, it lowered its head and quietly entered the water and disappeared' (*The Scotsman*, 5 June 1934).

This is one of the most significant of all the land accounts and is spoilt only by the lack of corroboration. Miss Munro had only recently joined the staff at the Lodge and no one else was up at that time on the Sunday morning. In view of the early hour and her new surroundings, she did not like to wake her employers, Mr and Mrs Arthur Pimley.

When Mr and Mrs Pimley did hear what Miss Munro had seen they were understandably rather irritated at having missed such a unique experience. At about 9 o'clock in the morning they walked down to the beach and found 'On rather heavy shingle an impression which might have been caused by a huge body and in the centre of the indentation was a branch which appeared to have been pressed into the gravel' (*The Scotsman*, 5 June 1934).

With the exception of a land sighting claimed in July 1934 by Mr Ian J. Matheson of Fort Augustus, who said he saw a large animal on the shore near Glendoe Sawmill, nobody appears to have seen any further terrestrial excursions by the animals until 1960.

Why this sudden shyness of the animals? The volume of disturbance caused by steadily increasing traffic could have something to do with it. After 1933 and 1934 the animals had to adapt to a new and much noisier atmosphere, which might have dampened any instincts to come ashore. It is significant that when, in 1960, another animal was seen out of the water it was on the Horseshoe stretch of shoreline, where there is no road and no disturbance.

At about 3.30 on the afternoon of Sunday 28 February 1960, Mr Torquil MacLeod, a dedicated 'monster-hunter' engaged on a private expedition sponsored by Sir Charles Dixon, was driving south about two and a half miles south of Invermoriston.

He was glancing across the loch to the rugged, circular fall of scree which gives that area the name 'Horseshoe' when he saw something large and dark moving on the narrow beach. Having stopped the car and focused his binoculars on the object he found himself looking at a huge animal lying partly out of the water. A few hours later he wrote the following letter to Constance Whyte:

Altourie,
Blackfold,
Inverness.

Sunday, February 28, 1960.

Dear Mrs Whyte

I have had my first hint of success today! I have seen the L.N.M. at a range of one mile through $\times 8$ glasses in broad daylight (raining). It was half ashore and I had a clear view of it for nine minutes during which time its neck moved from side to side, the animal eventually turning itself suddenly to the left in a sort of U shape and flopping into deep water (which I deduced from the fact that it did not re-appear or leave any wake, only ripples where it went in.)

I am as excited as a schoolboy about it all and this sighting has abolished the last faint doubts I had that it may have been some cognate form of animal.

As it turned I had a clear view of its left fore flipper which is grey in colour, spade-shaped and devoid of any markings which might indicate toes or claws, i.e., it is therefore a flipper and not a foot.

Most unfortunately the head is too small to show any details at such a distance and in any case, except for about one second as it turned, it was facing more or less directly away from me all the time...

I confess to being rather appalled at its size, somehow the descriptions have not quite sunk in, or perhaps I have become too familiar with them, but there is no doubt that the individual animal I saw this afternoon was of the order of 40/60 feet in length, and I did not at any time, alas, see its tail as the body was at no time completely clear of the water. It looked, as other witnesses have said, like elephant's skin but I got the impression that the back was more rounded than humped, looking at it end on from behind with the animal resting at an an angle on the shore, i.e., with its forepart higher than its hindquarters. This may of course have been due to

99

its posture or even an effect of light and shadows such as there was.

I had a colour cine camera with me but no telephoto lens, so I reserved what film I had loaded in case it approached. I gave it half an hour after its disappearance but saw no evidence of it or its wash and so came home.

It must be the most formidable sight at close quarters. As my glasses are graticulated and I took the most careful note of marks on the shore at each end of the animal I will be able to estimate a minimum length when I have worked out my graticulation tables . . .

Mr MacLeod described the animal's head and neck as being similar to an elephant's trunk which kept moving from side to side and up and down. A pair of large paddles were visible at the rear end and, as he describes in the letter, as the animal lurched around to enter the water one of its fore paddles came into view. The minimum length, he calculated from Almanac tables, was fifty feet, excluding the tail, which he did not see.

The value of this account lies in the weight one can attach to the observations of a trained watcher and experienced naturalist such as Mr MacLeod. He had the animal clearly in view for nine minutes and studied it closely; his report reflects the care and accuracy of his observations. The one outstanding point of difference between this and all the other descriptions of creatures seen on land is the size. The animal Mr MacLeod saw and measured so carefully was huge – over sixty feet long if we include the tail. In contrast, all the estimates of size in the previous land accounts describe comparatively small or medium-sized animals. Mr Cruickshank described a twenty to twenty-five foot animal; the Spicers put the length at about twenty-five feet and Arthur Grant saw a fifteen to twenty foot animal. This perhaps suggests that it is the smaller and younger animals which are more inclined to come ashore.

One further semi-land sighting deserves mention here. On 6 June 1963 six expedition members of the Loch Ness Investigation Bureau (see Chapter 7) observed and studied through binoculars at a range of just over two miles a large object which moved through shallow water and eventually remained stationary on or just off the beach at a point on the south shore op-

26. Sketch by Margaret Munro of the animal she saw on Borlum Beach in June 1934.

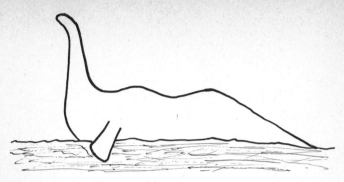

27. Borlum Bay near Fort Augustus. Arrowed is the spot where the animal Margaret Munro saw was situated. The photograph is taken from the position from which she was watching.

28. (*left*) Artist's impression of the creature Torquil MacLeod observed hauled on to a beach in February 1960. (Alan Jones)

29. The wake thrown up by one of the animals, photographed by the Lowrie family from their yacht *Finola* on 7 August 1960. (R. H. Lowrie)

30. One of the Loch Ness Investigation Bureau's early expeditions with a camera rig mounted on the battlements of Urquhart Castle. (Tim Dinsdale)

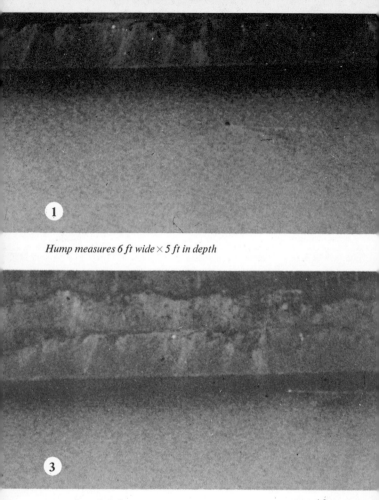

Hump measures 6 ft wide × 5 ft in depth

turns abruptly left.   SPEED 10 M.P.H

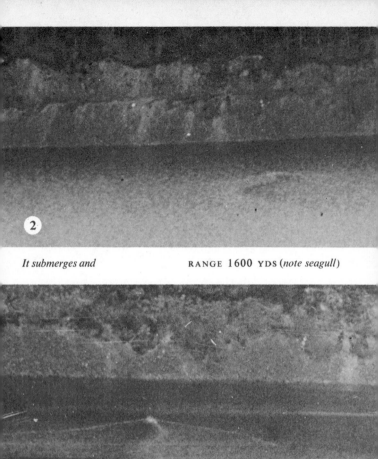

It submerges and RANGE 1600 YDS (*note seagull*)

A 14 × 5 ft boat with 5 h.p. outboard provides a comparison

32. The L N I B camera tower on Sandy Beach, opposite Urquhart Castle, in the summer of 1964. (F. W. Holiday)

33. The 35 mm cine camera rig at Achnahannet, fitted with a 36-inch lens and with two still cameras mounted on either wing; the whole apparatus had a range of several miles. (Peter Hodge)

34. One of the mobile camera rigs deployed by the Investigation Bureau during fine weather. (Peter Hodge)

35. Loch Ness, summer 1970. Sonar and hydrophone equipment being deployed in drums in Urquhart Bay. (F. W. Holiday)

36. The tiny one-man submarine *Viperfish* being lowered into the loch during the hectic summer of 1969. In the background is the Vickers Oceanics craft *Pisces*. (*Daily Mirror*)

37. Monster-hunting activity in Urquhart Bay, August 1969. The miniature submarine *Viperfish* is pictured in the foreground with veteran monster-hunter Tim Dinsdale aboard his photographic patrol boat *Water Horse* in the background. (Ivor Newby)

38. American sonar engineer Robert Love operating underwater sweeps of the loch aboard the motor vessel *Rangitea* in the summer of 1969. (Peter Hodge)

39. Wing-Commander Ken Wallis piloting his autogyro on patrol over Loch Ness in the summer of 1970. (Ivor Newby)

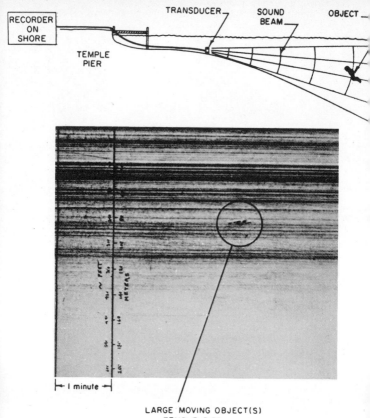

LARGE MOVING OBJECT(S)
TEMPLE PIER
LOCH NESS, SCOTLAND
21 SEPTEMBER, 1970, 18:10 BST
FIRST CONTACT, DISTANCE APPROXIMATELY 250 feet

40. Sonar target picked up off Temple Pier, Urquhart Bay, by the Academy of Applied Science team in September 1970. (Klein Associates)

41. The dramatic underwater photograph obtained in August 1972 by the Academy of Applied Science team, showing what is believed to be the flipper and roughly textured side of one of the animals. The 'flipper' is estimated to be six to eight feet in length. (Academy of Applied Science)

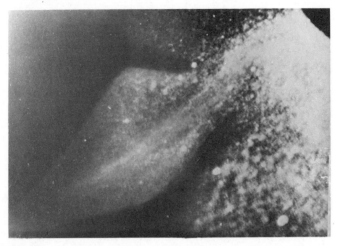

42. Bob Rines, president of the American Academy of Applied Science (*left*), with Tim Dinsdale, leading British monster-hunter.

"... the animal(s) has(have) a dimensional extent of approximately 20 to 30 feet as determined from the length of the echo..."
P. SKITZKI, RAYTHEON CO.

"...about 30 feet long...with projections or humps."
R. EIDE, SIMRAD

"...real...large...moving...trace indicating the possibility that the creature has several segments, body sections or projections such as humps.
...there are at least TWO large things moving."
M. KLEIN, KLEIN ASSOC.

"...another large marine animal, or a school of fish."
"A sudden echo protuberance exists with a dimension of about 10 feet...would appear to be an appendage..."
P. SKITZKI, RAYTHEON CO.

"...target projections...are 5 feet or more apart."
I. DYER, OCEAN ENG. DEPT., M.I.T.

"...large object is intruding into the zone of beam coverage!"
J. V. BOUYOUCOS, HYDROACOUSTICS

"number of small fish running away from a larger moving creature."
M. KLEIN, KLEIN ASSOC.

"school of fish"
P. SKITZKI, RAYTHEON

2:10 A.M. —

LOCH NESS, SCOTLAND
AUGUST 8, 1972, 1:40 A.M. —

WATER SURFACE

SLOPING BOTTOM
RAYTHEON DE-725C SONAR

35ft   30ft   60ft   90ft   45ft   120ft   150ft

5ft   30ft

EDGERTON STROBE-CAMERA

© 1972 ACAD. APPLIED SCIENCE, BELMONT, MASS.,
LOCH NESS INVESTIGATION BUR., LONDON, ENGLAND

43. The sonar chart from the night of 8 August 1972, when two large objects swam past the underwater camera, with analyses of the traces.
(Academy of Applied Science)

44. Artist's impression of the long-necked plesiosaur, a marine dinosaur thought to have been extinct for about seventy million years and a contender for the identity of the animals of Loch Ness. (Trustees of the British Museum, Natural History)

45. Loch Ness, 1973. The Academy's specially designed underwater camera rig is prepared for lowering into the loch.

46. The underwater camera station currently in operation at Loch Ness being lowered into Urquhart Bay. It consists of cameras and bright flashing lights which are automatically triggered by sonar, linked through a computer system, if any object larger than twenty feet passes within range. Dr Rines in foreground.

47. The coelacanth, a fish thought to have been extinct for seventy million years until a live specimen was caught off the coast of Madagascar in 1938. (Trustees of the British Museum, Natural History)

48. **Dr** Robert Rines (right) with the Edgerton underwater strobe
camera which took both the 1972 'flipper' photograph and the
1975 series. The upper cylinder houses a 16mm. camera, the lower
cylinder a strobe light which flashes periodically at the same time
as the camera takes a single photograph. The camera was designed
by **Dr** Harold Edgerton of the Massachusetts Institute of
Technology – the famous 'Papa Flash' in the Jacques Cousteau
adventures.

posite Urquhart Castle. The eye-witnesses gained the impression of a long, slim appendage, and 16 mm. cine film was shot of it. This film was subsequently analysed by the Joint Air Reconnaissance Intelligence Centre of the Royal Air Force, which reported that the object was five feet in height and seventeen feet in length. The extreme range made further evaluation impossible.

*

We have about a dozen reports of the animals being seen on land over a sixty-year period. In view of our almost total ignorance about these animals it is rather futile to try to speculate why they come ashore. It has been suggested that it may be connected with their breeding habits, or that it is some hereditary instinct left over from previous generations which used to be truly amphibious. This would seem most feasible, particularly since we now know from the latest underwater photographs that their paddles or flippers are large and strong and look capable of providing some rudimentary form of land propulsion.

One wonders whether there will ever again be a land sighting like the Spicers' or Arthur Grant's, when one of these lumbering anachronisms stumbles into twentieth-century man's environment and on to his machinery. It is, if nothing else, a stimulating consideration for the motorist at Loch Ness!

Chapter Seven

The Net Closes

Early on the morning of Saturday 23 April 1960 an English aeronautical engineer named Tim Dinsdale set out for a drive along the shores of Loch Ness which was to change the course of his whole life. He was 'monster-hunting', a harmless enough pursuit, indulged in by scores of people before him, which can be quite enjoyable so long as it is not undertaken too strenuously.

However, Mr Dinsdale had been taking it very seriously. For months past he had researched the subject and for the previous five days of his private expedition he had been rising at dawn and setting out to patrol various sectors of the loch – so far without any success. On this particular morning he was accustoming himself to an emotion which is rather common among monster-hunters – disappointment, since this was the final day of his expedition. The next morning he had to return to his home in the South and pick up once again the rather more humdrum routine of his profession.

At about 8.30 he decided to cut short his vigil opposite the Horseshoe and return to Foyers for breakfast. Half an hour later he was passing through Upper Foyers village and nearing his hotel. At this point the road is about 300 feet above the loch and set some distance back from it. Trees obscure the water for much of the way but there is the occasional break bringing Foyers Bay and the surrounding loch into view. It was while coasting past one of these gaps that Tim Dinsdale looked out across the loch and noticed something on the surface about 1,300 yards away. In his book *Loch Ness Monster* (page 100) he describes what then happened:

Unhurriedly I stopped the car and raising my binoculars, focused them carefully upon it. The object was perfectly clear and now quite large, and although when first I had seen it, it lay sideways on, during the few seconds I had taken with the binoculars it seemed to have turned away from me. It lay motionless on the water, a long oval shape, a distinct mahogany colour and on the left flank a huge dark blotch could be seen, like the dapple on a cow. For some reason it reminded me of the back of an African buffalo – it had fullness and girth and stood well above the water, and although I could see it from end to end there was no visible sign of a dorsal fin upon it; and then, abruptly, it began to move. I saw ripples break away from the further end and I knew at once I was looking at the extraordinary humped back of some huge living creature!

Mr Dinsdale turned to the 16 mm. Bolex cine camera standing on its tripod in the car next to him and began to film the animal. It swam away across the loch following an erratic course and throwing out an extensive V-shaped wake. It was slowly submerging, and 200 to 300 yards from the far shore it abruptly changed direction and started swimming south, parallel to the shore. By now it was almost beneath the surface and Mr Dinsdale decided on a desperate gamble. He was running short of film – so far he had been filming for four minutes – and needed to get closer to the shore in case the animal turned and headed back across the loch. He therefore stopped filming and drove madly on, down through Lower Foyers, across a field and to the water's edge. When he got there the loch surface was calm. The animal had returned to the depths.

It was this film, just fifty feet of celluloid, which heralded a new phase in the saga of the 'Monster'. For the first time since the 1930s somebody had taken a film, and a good film, of one of the animals. Suddenly the star's wrinkles disappeared. 'Nessie' was firmly back in the news, and this was a come-back which was going to last.

Although at first Mr Dinsdale tried to keep the film a secret and hoped to show it to the scientific community in private, the press eventually got to hear about it. On 13 June 1960 the *Daily Mail* published details and stills from it. That evening Mr Dinsdale appeared on BBC Television's *Panorama* and the film was shown. Within a few days a large response was appearing and Mr Dinsdale received mail from all over the country from people expressing their support for and belief in these animals. Some observed how similar the object in the film was to something they themselves had seen in the loch.

Coincidentally, at about the same time as the film was given its first public showing, preparations were being made for another serious expedition to the loch. Thanks originally to Constance Whyte's *More Than a Legend* and, more particularly, to the encouragement of the phenomenon's only faithful zoological champion at the time, Dr Denys W. Tucker, a Principal Scientific Officer at the British Museum of Natural History, a team of thirty graduates and undergraduates from the universities of Oxford and Cambridge embarked on 27 June for a month-long investigation. Their aim was to accomplish the first scientific survey of Loch Ness to determine whether it is ecologically capable of supporting a colony of large animals, and also to carry out photographic surveillance and echo-sounding sweeps.

Unfortunately, for reasons which will be outlined below, Dr Tucker was prevented from leading this expedition in person. However, under the organization of Cambridge graduate Peter Baker, the party took to the field with their collection of cameras and a Marconi echo sounder. During the course of the search a brief sighting of a ten-foot-long hump was made on Sunday 10 July by Mr Bruce Ing off Achnahannet, and several unusual echo traces were recorded. Of these the most interesting occurred on 4 July, when an object was tracked as it dived at speed from the surface to sixty feet and back up again.

The expedition made one important discovery, large shoals of char at a depth of about 100 feet, the existence of which had previously only been rumoured. The overall finding was that Loch Ness is quite capable of supporting a group of large predatory animals.*

*

*Full reports on the expedition findings appeared in *The Scotsman* of 12, 13 and 14 September 1960.

We now come to one of two potentially very sensitive topics in the Loch Ness story, that of Dr Denys Tucker and his dismissal from his post at the British Museum of Natural History in June 1960. Suffice it to say here that, at the time, both the press and Dr Tucker suggested that his involvement in the Loch Ness investigation and his publicly expressed belief in the animals' existence were at least a contributory factor in the confused circumstances of his departure from the Museum.

Dr Tucker had held a Museum post for eleven years and is an internationally respected expert on eels. For several years before 1960 he had vigorously pursued the Loch Ness question and had lectured on it to leading societies and at universities, though not without attempts by some university authorities to prevent the lectures. He records in a letter dated 9 January 1960 the reception he received when giving a talk entitled 'Loch Ness – the Case for Investigation' to a distinguished zoological club in London. For obvious reasons, names are omitted.

At the dinner prior to the meeting, several members made snide remarks: 'So you're going to tell us how to catch the Monster, hee, hee!' ... in the half hour discussion which followed [the talk], there was only one hostile critic, — —, who sneered at Gould and ridiculed almost all the evidence and said it was clearly a seal. To my great delight he was practically lynched by the rest of the audience and howled down; Professor —, for example, was shouting: 'You shut your — mouth! What the — hell do you know about it?'

From which it would seem that interest and support were germinating even amongst the boffins. This did not, however, save Dr Tucker in June. *The Times* reported: 'Dr Tucker said that when he told the museum authorities that he was going to investigate the Loch Ness Monster as a holiday task, he was told not to do this. He replied that they could not stop him unless they dismissed him and if they did there would be a great fuss in the Press.' Questions were, in fact, asked in Parliament.

*

On the afternoon of Sunday 7 August 1960 one of the animals was independently watched by a party of people on land and by a family aboard a yacht, who also took photographs of the disturbance it made as it passed them. The shore group included Torquil MacLeod (who six months earlier had had the land sighting at the Horseshoe), his wife and a Mr and Mrs Seddon-Smith from Australia. Aboard the forty-foot motor yacht *Finola* were company director Mr R. H. Lowrie and his family from Newcastle upon Tyne. Their log reads:

4.15 p.m. Brian on watch. Family below for Sunday lunch. Brian enquired: 'What is this monster supposed to look like? There is something coming up astern.' All hands on deck witness a curious form coming up astern between six and ten knots looking like a couple of ducks, occasionally submerging, and a neck-like protrusion breaking surface. The Monster – nothing less. As it came abeam we were fascinated, so much so that it had passed to starboard before anyone remembered that we had an old camera aboard. After about ten minutes it swung away to starboard towards Aldourie Point and some photographs were then taken. It swam quickly causing considerable disturbance and showing a large area of green and brown, and proceeded on a collision reciprocal course to our own.

A hurried family conference unanimously decided that something sinister was approaching, and that we should alter course to avoid a close contact.

From the shore and through binoculars Mr MacLeod could see distinct rhythmic splashes as if made by paddle action. The animal's speed was estimated at eight to nine knots. Although the photographs show only the long V-wake of the animal, the Lowrie family estimated its length to be similar to that of their boat, forty feet.

*

The year 1961 is notable for the inception of an organization which, in its lifetime, was to be the subject of almost as much local controversy as that generated on a wider scale by its quarry. This was the Loch Ness Investigation Bureau.

In August 1960, as a result of the new spate of interest after Tim Dinsdale's film, two well-known naturalists decided to take up the cudgels in an attempt to see what practical help could be extracted from within the establishment's ambidextrous defences. Accordingly, the two naturalists, Sir Peter Scott, son of the great Antarctic explorer and eminent founder of the Wildfowl Trust, and Mr Richard Fitter, Council Member of the Fauna Preservation Society, approached a Member of Parliament and requested him to try to get Government assistance for 'a flat-out attempt to find what exactly is in Loch Ness.'

The M.P. they chose was Highland laird Mr David James, M.B.E., D.S.C., Antarctic traveller, author and famous wartime escaper. At first Mr James eschewed involvement in such a singular subject, but once he had read *More Than a Legend* his curiosity and crusading spirit were aroused. In his booklet *Loch Ness Investigation* he wrote: 'It seemed to me quite evident that a massive case was going by default simply because the already available evidence had not been sufficiently widely disseminated, particularly to those people who are best qualified to form a judgment, namely the professional zoologists.'

Although Mr James declined to raise the matter in Parliament as Mr Hector Hughes had done several years before, he soon became one of the driving forces in the new campaign for recognition of the animals' existence.

One of the group's first acts was to convene a special meeting in London in April 1961 to discuss the Loch Ness phenomenon. It was attended by five leading scientists; they heard evidence from Mr and Mrs Lowrie, Torquil MacLeod, Peter Baker and the Rev. Mr William Dobb (who had a good hump sighting in August 1960) and saw Mr Peter Macnab's photograph and Tim Dinsdale's film. The proceedings of this meeting remain confidential, presumably to protect the distinguished panel from ridicule. After much deliberation, they decided that there was a prima facie case for investigation and that it was a subject worthy of submission to the Royal Society for investigation and to the Royal Navy for any assistance it could provide. However, none of these resolutions produced any positive results, which is understandable when one considers what one very prominent scientist said about the evidence he had seen: 'Absurd as it may seem I am forced to believe that it is actually more likely that what was seen was some artificial body,

107

perhaps some wirelessly controlled submergible model "monster" operated by some super "leg-puller" who has been playing his tricks for some ten years or more.'

This approaches the realms of the lowest cartoon humour, which frequently depicts a team of kilted Scottish frogmen swimming in Loch Ness wearing a 'Monster' outfit rather like an aquatic pantomime horse.

Notwithstanding this lack of official support, the Bureau for Investigating the Loch Ness Phenomena Ltd (as it was originally called) was formally incorporated on 20 March 1962, with David James, Constance Whyte, Peter Scott and Richard Fitter as its directors. It was a registered charity which proposed to act primarily as a clearing-house for information and secondly as an active research body. It was decided that any profits accruing at the end of its existence should be donated to the World Wildlife Fund and the Council for Nature.

The Bureau's first foray into the active role of 'monster-hunting' took place in October 1962, when, with the assistance of Associated Television, two ex-wartime Government searchlights, each with a range of six miles, were taken to the loch and played across its dark waters every night for two weeks. The team's hope was that the animals might be attracted by the beam. On the night of 19 October one of the searchlight operators, Mr Michael Spear, observed a 'finger-like object' standing six to eight feet out of the water, caught in the beam. Earlier that afternoon seven of the twenty-four expedition members saw and filmed a 'long, dark shape', moving through the waters of Urquhart Bay at a range of about 200 yards, which was visibly disturbing fish. Subsequent analysis by the Royal Air Force's Central Reconnaissance Establishment verified the visible length to be about eight feet, and added: 'It is not wave effect, but has some solidity, is dark in tone and glistens.'

A committee which studied the expedition's findings in November of that year and which consisted of a barrister, a marine biologist, and two naturalists (none of whom was connected with the Bureau) found: 'That there is some unidentified animate object in Loch Ness which, if it be a mammal, amphibian, reptile, fish or mollusc of any known order, is of such size as to be worthy of careful scientific examination and identification.'

A twenty-minute ATV programme, *Report on the Loch Ness Monster*, broadcast the panel's findings but made little impact on either public or press, except the *Inverness Courier*, which headlined: 'There IS a Monster in Loch Ness – Expedition's Findings Accepted by Experts – Highlanders Vindicated.' It is the sort of newspaper headline one dreams about, but, as with so much of importance which occurred during this period, it slipped by unnoticed.

Apart from the Bureau, other teams were also in the field in 1962. Lieutenant-Colonel H. G. Hasler, D.S.O., O.B.E., (leader of the 'Cockleshell Heroes' who in 1942 carried out a daring canoe raid on German ships in Bordeaux harbour), and a team of forty volunteers maintained a two-month watch from the beginning of June from boats and from the shore. Hydrophones, the underwater listening device, were used, and several low-frequency tapping noises were recorded which seemed animal-like in nature. Two brief sightings were made, one of which was witnessed by Commander Sir Peter Ogilvy-Wedderburn, Bt, when three small humps appeared in Urquhart Bay at a range of about fifty feet.

In July, Dr Peter Baker led another team from Cambridge University which put in nearly five hundred hours of surface observation as well as undertaking another sonar search. Three sightings of unidentified objects were made. Four boats were equipped with very sensitive echo sounders and in the course of a number of sweeps along the loch three underwater contacts were picked up, one of which immediately preceded a surface sighting.

*

It would be both time-consuming and tedious to catalogue all of the many things which occurred at Loch Ness in the mid-1960s, a period of intense activity involving scores of expeditions, ranging in size from the lone camper with a snapshot camera to the progressively more sophisticated Bureau expeditions. A broad outline of the events will be given here. (For a more detailed account, see Tim Dinsdale's latest book,

Project Waterhorse, Routledge and Kegan Paul, 1975.)

In 1963 about fifty Bureau volunteers spent two weeks at the loch at the beginning of June, living in caravans and tents at Achnahannet. Ten camera stations were established at strategic positions around the loch and, with the assistance of local residents, were manned from 4 a.m. to 10 p.m. every day. On 13 June, the day before the expedition packed up, film was shot of what appears to have been one of the animals from a camera position at Urquhart Castle. By coincidence, a reporter and a photographer from the Aberdeen *Evening Express* were present during the sighting. The reporter, Miss Jay Dawson, wrote:

When we arrived at the expedition site, everybody in the party was in a state of excitement, peering towards the calm, misty loch through binoculars. At first I could see nothing. Then, about a quarter of the way out from the shore and half a mile from where I was standing I saw a dark object bobbing up and down in the water.

It was moving slightly and seemed to be playing around. I could scarcely believe my eyes. Unfortunately it was too far away from me to make out definite details but I'm certain it was not any normal-sized loch creature. I have never seen anything like it in the loch before and I am convinced it was the Monster.

When we reached a better vantage point the Monster had disappeared below the surface, creating a disturbance. As I watched I overheard one of the expedition cameramen, who had rushed to the scene before us and got pictures, say that he had a 'head and neck in the can'. [*Evening Express*, 13 June 1963]

The cameraman's optimism was unforunately misplaced; the film was largely ruined by a heavy heat haze which impaired clarity. However, when the expedition's findings were put to another panel of independent experts in London in the autumn of 1963 they stated: 'We are impressed by the fact that distinct progression along the surface can be observed in the film and was reported by observers. There was turbulence around the object and a streak behind it ... If this was an animate object, it was an animal of a species wholly unknown to any of us.'

The 1964 expedition took a rather different form. Instead of concentrating a lot of watching into a two-week period, it was decided to keep two camera stations going from mid-May to

October, manned by successive groups of volunteers. With the financial and physical assistance of Associated Television (its deputy chairman, Mr Norman Collins, had recently joined the Bureau as its Chairman) two impressive long-range camera rigs were built, consisting of a 35 mm. cine camera fitted with a 36-inch lens with the magnifying power to pick out a nine-inch object at a range of up to two miles, and two ex-R.A.F. 'still' cameras with 20-inch lenses, all operated from one control. One of these rigs was mounted on a platform on the ramparts of Urquhart Castle and the other was placed on an observation tower erected on a beach on the southern shore almost opposite the Castle.

In fact neither of the Bureau rigs shot any film in 1964 but a visitor with a small 8 mm. cine camera succeeded in doing so. In the latter part of May, Mr Peter Hodge and his wife Pauline embarked on a private expedition inspired by Tim Dinsdale's film and book. At about 8.15 on the morning of 21 May, Mr Hodge clambered out of their tent, which was in the field at Achnahannet used the previous year by the Bureau. He described to me what happened:

I was going over to the car to get the cameras when I noticed a pole-like object sticking up out of the flat calm surface of the water, just above the tree line. It was just like a long pole. I couldn't make out any detail because I was looking into the sun. I called to Pauline and grabbed the cameras. Unfortunately I slammed the car door shut and the object immediately disappeared. A second later a wash started to track rapidly across the loch with a black dot at the head of it. I took several colour slides and Pauline started filming it with the cine camera.

It went right across the loch and then turned left and Pauline noticed that on the left hand side there were splashes rather like a paddling effect . . . I would say that the neck must have been all of four feet tall when I first saw it. The speed as it travelled across the loch was about five to eight m.p.h.

The animal's progress was also watched by four students camped in the field who came piling out of their tent when Peter Hodge shouted to his wife.

Later that day they reported the event to the Bureau expedition at Urquhart Castle and were invited to join the organization. Since then they have been amongst the most dedicated members of the 'monster-hunting' fraternity. Strangely enough, later that same evening they had another unusual experience. A Bureau member, Ivor Newby, another 'monster-hunter' of long standing and wide experience, had arrived at Achnahannet with a Sighting Report Form for the Hodges. Peter Hodge again describes what happened:

It was rather a dull evening but the loch was still calm. I was talking to Ivor and suddenly realized he wasn't paying the slightest attention to what I was saying but was staring at the loch. I followed his gaze and saw that there were two dark objects just under or touching the surface quite near to where I had seen the neck in the morning. They clearly couldn't be rocks because there aren't any there. It is about 200 yards out from the shore and the water is over 100 feet deep. Each object was about ten feet in length. Ivor grabbed his camera and hurdled over a fence to get down the hill. I followed but caught my foot and did an almost complete somersault in the air . . . we shot some film but it was now getting so gloomy that we eventually lost sight of them . . . Nothing came out on this film.

In 1964 the Bureau moved its headquarters to Achnahannet, where it was to remain until the end of 1972, when it was finally forced to close down. A new watching policy was adopted. A main camera rig at headquarters was, in theory, manned continuously throughout the hours of daylight of the summer-long annual expeditions. In addition, when the prevailing weather was suitable, camera-vans were dispatched to vantage points along the loch's northern shore. Odd sequences of film were shot in both 1965 and 1966 but despite several thousand hours of watching through depressingly damp and windy summers, convincing close-up photography continued to evade the steadily expanding numbers of Bureau volunteers.

The major development of 1966 concerned Tim Dinsdale's 1960 film. Since taking it he had made many further trips to the loch in the hope of obtaining the final, definitive proof of the animals' existence, but he had had no further sightings. In 1961 he had given up his job and was thereafter totally committed to the search.

112

Encouraged by the Royal Air Force's Joint Air Reconnaissance Intelligence Centre's success at analysing their films,* David James gave them Mr Dinsdale's film for evaluation. J.A.R.I.C. is an internationally respected photographic and film analytical authority. Every frame of the original Dinsdale film was optically enlarged and examined, and in January 1966 the findings were reported. As an example of the degree of accuracy attained in such an analysis, J.A.R.I.C. estimated the length of the boat which Mr Dinsdale had filmed immediately after filming the animal (to provide a comparison with an object of known size and power) at 13.3 feet. In fact its length was 14 feet. Bearing in mind that they were working from the tiny area of a 16 mm. film negative and the range was over a mile, such accuracy is most impressive and allows for no reasonable criticism of their findings.

The Intelligence Centre's experts stated in an official report later published by Her Majesty's Stationery Office that the object filmed was not a surface craft or a submarine, 'which leaves the conclusion that it probably is an animate object.'

It was, the report said, standing about three feet above the water when first sighted, and 'Even if the object is relatively flat bellied, the normal body "rounding" in nature would suggest that there is at least two feet under the water from which it may be deduced that a cross section through the object would be NOT LESS than six feet wide and five feet high.' It was also said that the original hump was between twelve and sixteen feet in length and was travelling at between seven and ten m.p.h. The report further stated that whereas the boat Mr Dinsdale filmed showed a distinguishable boat shape, the object had no such shape; therefore the possibility that it was a boat is completely ruled out.

In 1972 Mr Dinsdale's film, like Colonel R. K. Wilson's photograph, was sent to the American computer-enhancement experts who worked on the *Apollo* moon photographs. Their computer scanner studied each frame of the film and found that, very briefly, two further parts of the body break the sur-

* In 1965 they studied a film showing two wakes moving at first together and then obliquely to each other.

face in addition to the main hump. This had been invisible under normal projection arrangements.

One film was taken in 1966, but again not by the Bureau. Inverness housewife Mrs Margaret Edward saw and filmed an object on the surface near Abriachan for about one minute. She saw a big hump and what resembled a tail, but the 8 mm. film, according to experts who studied it, only revealed a disturbance in the water and suggested the presence of something solid.

By 1967 American interest and involvement in the search had grown to such an extent that without it the Investigation Bureau would undoubtedly have collapsed. Professor Roy Mackal, a Professor of Biochemistry at the University of Chicago, had been appointed a Director of the Bureau and was gathering support in the U.S.A. Constance Whyte had, by this time, resigned from the organization's board. In the spring, the Field Enterprises Educational Corporation of Chicago made a donation of $20,000 to the research fund, and the Highlands and Island Development Board gave £1,000 in recognition of the Bureau's services to the local tourist trade. The donations made it possible to invest in more long-range cameras, which finally made contact with the animals during the 1967 expedition.

On 22 May, Bureau watcher Les Durkin filmed a disturbance and two low humps moving through the water near Invermoriston. J.A.R.I.C. reported: 'The length of the disturbed areas are 50 feet, 65 feet, 38 feet and 45 feet. Their speed from left to right is approximately six knots, and they have portions raised some two feet above water level.'

On 13 June, another Bureau cameraman, Dick Raynor, watched and filmed an extensive V-shaped wake moving out of Dores Bay from his position near Abriachan. As he filmed it, the pleasure boat *Scott II* came into view and proceeded parallel with it for a short distance. J.A.R.I.C. reported on this, having optically enlarged it up to 38 times magnification: 'It is probable that the mean speed of the object is not less than five m.p.h, and a possible length for that part of the object which seems to break the surface is in the order of seven feet.'

Underwater Eyes

In 1968, while the Bureau carried on its traditional pattern of research, a new group arrived to make their contribution to the investigation. In the spring Professor D. G. Tucker, Head of the Department of Electronic and Electrical Engineering at the University of Birmingham, with Dr Hugh Braithwaite and Dr D. J. Creasey, visited the loch and decided it would make an ideal testing ground for a new type of sonar apparatus they had designed. The team returned for two weeks in August and trials began. The sonar equipment was operated from Temple Pier, and a narrow beam was directed out under the waters of Urquhart Bay. A sonar pulse was transmitted every ten seconds, and a camera was aligned to photograph each resulting display on the oscillascope screen.

At about 4.30 p.m. on 28 August,* the sonar picked up an echo from 'a large object' dubbed 'A', estimated to be about fifty metres in length, rising from the loch floor at a range of 0.8 kilometres. For the next ten minutes this object moved in and out of the beam; it dived and rose at a rate of up to 120 feet per minute and accelerated to a speed of about nine knots. During this period it was joined by two other objects, 'B' and 'C'. Object B was almost certainly a shoal of fish; this was clear from its echo characteristics. Object C, however, behaved in a truly amazing fashion by normal animal standards. It reached a speed of fifteen knots and a diving velocity of 450 feet per minute. The scientists' report continues: 'Since objects A and C are clearly comprised of animals, is it possible they could be fish? The high rate of ascent and descent makes this seem very unlikely, and fishery biologists we have consulted cannot suggest what fish they might be.' Object C was long in the vertical plane and short horizontally, suggesting a streamlined object in the act of diving.

Although Professor Tucker made no claims about the identity of these strange objects, his results were ruthlessly attacked in the distinguished scientific journal *Nature* (Vol. 220, 28 December 1968), which stated that 'there is little reason to take

* As described in *New Scientist*, 19 December 1968.

seriously the claims of Dr Braithwaite and Professor Tucker to have found a monster.'

Once again one sees the scientific establishment desperately trying to defend its territory from the possibility that something exists which it cannot understand. Professor Tucker is an eminent sonar engineer who clearly knows vastly more about his equipment than do the editors of *Nature*, who were not even able to get their basic facts correct in their criticism of the Birmingham results.

The Birmingham team carried out further work at the loch in both 1969 and 1970 but declined to publish any details of their findings.

Despite the scientific apathy shown in Britain towards the 1968 results, American scientists, who so often seem to have more initiative than the British variety, were taking a progressively larger interest in the investigation.

The summer of 1969 produced the greatest amount of activity at Loch Ness that there has ever been. Field Enterprises of America sponsored an unprecedentedly large Bureau expedition which involved a miniature submarine and the most comprehensive sonar search ever attempted. The publicity which all this inevitably attracted was augmented by a special investigation by the Independent Television News *News at Ten* programme and the *Daily Mail* newspaper. The latter sent their veteran chief reporter, Vincent Mulchrone, to the loch.

Unfortunately there was another hoax. Even more unfortunately, just as in 1933, the *Daily Mail* was on the receiving end. Three English gentlemen produced a giant bone which they claimed to have stumbled across one day when they were fishing. Actually, it was a portion of the discarded jaw bone of a blue whale which had formed part of a garden rockery in the grounds of a Yorkshire museum. Sadly for the *Daily Mail*, this fact emerged only after it had splashed pictures of the bone all over its main news pages.

Centrepiece of the summer's activity was the miniature yellow submarine *Viperfish*, designed, built and piloted by Mr Dan Taylor from Atlanta, Georgia. Its purpose was to home-in on any targets picked up by the sonar, which was being operated by American electronics expert Mr Robert Love from the chartered motor vessel *Rangitea*. In addition to *Viperfish* a Vickers Oceanics *Pisces* submersible was also at Loch Ness at this time to carry out underwater diving trials, and to tow a five-ton dummy monster around the loch. This was one of the props in the film *The Private Life of Sherlock Holmes*, which was being shot at Urquhart Castle. The model, at much emotional and financial cost to the film-makers, sank on its first outing.

Pisces made a number of dives, one of which reached a depth of 820 feet, seventy feet deeper than the loch's official maximum depth. At 750 feet it encountered a strange, whirlpool current, and elsewhere the crew noticed fish and eels with unusual colourings. Their most interesting experience from the 'monster-hunting' point of view came on an occasion when the craft was hovering fifty feet off the bottom in the main channel of the loch about 300 yards north of Urquhart Castle. A sonar target was picked up at a range of 600 feet and the submersible began to home-in on it. When it was 400 feet away the target moved and disappeared from the sonar screen and no further contact was made with it.

To add to the pandemonium, a film crew from the Walt Disney Film Company arrived, and under the direction of Mr Ken Peterson what was intended to be a TV colour documentary was shot. Back in 1949, Walt Disney himself actively considered the Loch Ness Monster as a subject for one of his nature films but shelved the idea. Rather regrettably, the 1969 filming resulted in a half-hour semi-serious production, *Man, Mysteries and Monsters*, starring a multi-coloured, decidedly moronic cartoon 'Monster' arguing indignantly with a doubtful commentator that he was not just the pink elephant of some over-lubricated Scotsman's dreams.

Meanwhile, the serious 'monster-hunt' was slowly getting under way. Dan Taylor was having some difficulty in adapting his craft for the dangerous task he had undertaken, and *Viperfish* never really proved effective. It was too small for the vastness of Loch Ness, and gave its intrepid pilot some heart-stopping moments, as, for instance, when the pressure hatch

117

was jolted partly open and water began to flood in, or when the whole two-ton craft was swirled right around by some unseen force whilst resting on the bottom.

Mounted on *Viperfish* was a biopsy dart fired by compressed air, with which it was hoped to recover a tiny portion of skin from one of the animals, allowing them to be identified. This dart had originally been introduced by Professor Roy Mackal several years previously, but when the press heard about it the result was a question in the House of Lords. Lord Kilmany asked Her Majesty's Government whether they were satisfied 'that any monsters that may chance to inhabit that loch will not be subjected to damage or assault?' The Joint Parliamentary Under-Secretary for Scotland, Lord Hughes, replied that he was satisfied, and went on to ignore a pointed question from Lord Hawke as to whether he would like to be 'potted' by an airgun to take samples of his tissue.

Extracts from this debate were broadcast to the *Apollo 11* astronauts on their pioneering journey to the moon. When the mayor of Palm Beach heard about it he stated consolingly that he would be honoured to have a lord lead an expedition to Lake Okeechobee!

For six weeks starting in September Bob Love and his team plodded up and down the loch at all hours of the day and night operating the specially adapted Honeywell sonar. Among a number of unusual contacts, one displayed all the characteristics of being caused by a very large animal when, on 10 October, an object was tracked for more than two minutes near Foyers.

It was unfortunate that this success did not occur a few weeks earlier when the joint ITN and *Daily Mail* expedition was presenting daily coverage of the investigation's progress. They had brought their own sonar team from the Plessey Company, which sat in the middle of the loch and piped 50 kilowatts of low-frequency 'pinging' into the water which reverberated along the loch's whole twenty-four-mile length and undoubtedly sent the animals to ground. No contacts were made and the viewing and reading public was disappointed.

*

The following year, 1970, Tim Dinsdale took on the job of directing the Bureau's surface watching whilst Bob Love continued his sonar investigation. This time he was assisted by Dr Robert Rines and a small team from the Academy of Applied Science of Boston, Massachusetts, a private organization set up in 1963 to look into unexplored areas of science and to foster cooperation between the applied sciences and other disciplines. Its president, Robert H. Rines, was first attracted by the Loch Ness mystery in 1958, when on a visit to Inverness he read *More Than a Legend*. At that time he discussed the possibility of an expedition with scientific colleagues, but the project remained dormant until, in 1969, he heard a lecture on the subject at the Massachusetts Institute of Technology by Professor Roy Mackal and decided to offer the Academy's assistance to the search.

An autogyro was also used in the hunt for the first time in 1970. Its designer and pilot, Wing-Commander Ken Wallis, completed a month's flying over the loch, but without any success. Sonar chief Bob Love continued his underwater sweeps and also experimented with hydrophone equipment. Microphones were suspended in various localities from large oil drums containing the recording equipment. In total, four unusual sets of noises were picked up which appeared to be animate in origin. Amongst them were what Professor Mackal describes as 'clicks and knocks' which followed a regular rhythmic beat and which stopped every time a boat approached.

September saw the arrival of Bob Rines and his team, which included Dr Martin Klein, designer of the Klein Associates high-frequency side-scan sonar. Also amongst their equipment was a delightful collection of 'lures', consisting of a provoking mixture of animal hormones which were fruitlessly trailed about the loch by the Academy team from Tim Dinsdale's boat *Water Horse*. However, their sonar was predictably more successful. On 21 September, the side-scan apparatus detected two large objects passing through its beam whilst it was lashed to the end of Temple Pier. A few moments later one of these objects passed back in the opposite direction, showing a reversed 'shape'. Two days later the side-scan transducer 'fish', which

119

sends out and receives the sonar signal, was towed from *Water Horse* in the Horseshoe region and several more contacts with large, moving underwater objects were made.

*

This is, by necessity, a very brief review of the many developments in the Loch Ness investigation during this period. So much happened during the late 1960s and early 1970s that it is impossible to dwell in any detail on individual events. Professor Roy Mackal has recently compiled his own book, *The Search at Loch Ness – The Evidence and What It Means,* which is due for publication shortly and which approaches the scientific investigations in an appropriately technical way. This review does, I hope, show that, from 1968 onwards, expeditions consistently succeeded in tracking large underwater objects on sonar. The essence of the criteria of scientific acceptance is surely the ability to repeat a result under controlled conditions. This has been done again and again in recent years at Loch Ness and yet no response has been forthcoming from official science.

As well as the serious side to this phase of the 'monster-hunt' there has, of course, been a continuation of the traditional light-hearted and at times bizarre spin-off from it. The presence of the Loch Ness Investigation Bureau's headquarters at Achnahannet, where an exhibition was open to visitors, attracted its share of the eccentric and the unusual. There was, for example, the man who claimed the loch was full of people from Venus and that the 'Monster' was a Venusian spaceship; or the character who believed it used to come out every night, fly around and eat human beings; or the annual bicycling visitor who would tell people he had found a 'Nessie-nest' and report this year's brood of eggs! The exhibition also attracted tens of thousands of other visitors. In 1971, for example, 50,000 people viewed the small display of photographs, maps and charts.

In 1961 it was reported that Mr Pietro Annigoni had been commissioned to paint the Monster, surely his most difficult assignment. The following year King Olav of Norway expressed special interest in the mystery when he visited Inverness.

A few years later the Bishop of Basutoland actually paid a special visit to the loch to look for the 'Monster'.

In 1960 an Inverness councillor suggested offering a £5,000 reward for the first authentic photograph leading to positive zoological classification of the animals. The Common Good Committee threw the idea out since it was 'not competent' to do such a thing. At the same time an Isle of Wight zoo owner announced that he was training two dogs to 'sniff the monster out'.

In 1966 a Mr Barry Watson of Bingley, Yorkshire, attempted to swim the length of Loch Ness. He was evidently not impressed by the animals' record of good behaviour since he had an escort in boats armed with harpoon guns. Had anything appeared and had the date been 1971, they could perhaps have been £1 million the richer; for in that year a large Scotch whisky company offered this figure as a reward to anyone who captured the 'Monster' and delivered it to them in London. Obviously they turned a publicity-hungry blind eye to the legal restrictions on any such action, but nevertheless they took out an insurance policy with Lloyds. At first, they had great difficulty in obtaining cover, since nobody knew the correct category for 'Nessie' – livestock, marine or agricultural? After procrastination for three weeks a policy was issued and Lloyds upheld its tradition of offering insurance for every contingency.

In July 1970 a lecturer in visceral physiology at a London college, Mr Douglas Drysdale, stated that any 'Monsters' in Loch Ness must have been killed by pollution. On the day he made his announcement two sightings were reported to the Loch Ness Investigation Bureau. During the British Week in Tokyo in 1969, Mr Donald Harden of the London Museum at Kensington gallantly offered to deliver a lecture on any requested subject. Unfortunately for him the Japanese wanted to hear about 'Nessie', and the Board of Trade had to tell the inquisitive hosts that the 'Monster' was still regarded as a myth and not the sort of 'cultural subject Mr Harden felt capable of discussing.' He eventually gave his talk on the history of the Tower of London.

A zenith of worldwide interest in the mystery seems to have been reached in 1969, no doubt as a result of all the lochside activity and publicity. At the end of the year, Encyclopaedia Britannica announced that Loch Ness was among the leaders in their table of the ten subjects of greatest public interest, judged by the number of requests they received for information.

The serious expeditions were not the only ones to succeed in tracking the animals on sonar. In March 1964 the Stornoway fishing boat *Girl Norma* picked up a thirty-foot-long object at a depth of about 250 feet. In August 1966 the British Medical Association motor yacht *Pharma* tracked a moving object on the surface on its radar. Mr Mike Amery, B.Sc., estimated it was about thirty feet long. In April 1969 the echo sounder of the trawler *Ha-Burn* detected a very large object over 700 feet down. Skipper James Runcie of Cullen said: 'There was definitely something unusual down there.' The following April the Fraserburgh trawler *Tea Rose* detected a large object rising through the water column at about seven knots. 'Never seen anything like it,' commented the skipper, Mr Charles Duthy.

There were a number of good surface sightings as well, though none of them occurred in view of the Loch Ness Investigation Bureau's cameras, or if they did nobody was looking at the right moment.

One evening in July 1963 two Dores men, Mr Dan McIntosh and Mr James Cameron, were fishing from a small boat about 200 yards off Tor Point. At about 10 o'clock they realized that the boat was rocking on the flat calm water. Suddenly the head and neck of one of the animals reared four to five feet out of the water only twenty to thirty yards away from them. A short way behind the neck was a small hump. A moment later it sank vertically out of sight, causing a commotion in the water. The two men continued to fish but found that the area had suddenly become sterile. Mr McIntosh later described the appearance of the animal to F. W. Holiday. He said the head was wide and very ugly and was a continuation of the curve of the neck, that is, it was not distinctly separate from the neck. He saw no features on the head but said that there was a hairy mane hanging off its neck. Colour was brownish-black.

The following account is taken from a Loch Ness Investigation Bureau Sighting Report Form of 1965 and is one of the most interesting written accounts of the thoughts and mental reactions of a person who quite unexpectedly comes across one of the animals. The author is Miss E. M. J. Keith, the headmistress of Rothienorman School:

My brother-in-law and I went out from Inverness to Dores on the beautiful evening of Tuesday, 30 March, with the intention of walking from Dores to Tor Point as I was interested in seeing the changing face of the countryide . . . There was a marvellous sunset with reflections of hills and red sky and the loch was as calm as a millpond . . . And then it happened! Paddling across the loch towards Dores and not very far out from the shore was this black creature. There was no commotion in the water. As it came in line with us the creature changed direction from crossing and proceeded down the middle of the loch. I was rooted to the spot for I had never seen anything like this before . . . That this was a living creature on the water there was no doubt, but of what species I had no idea. There was no lashing of the tail, though the big rings formed a large wake and continued to be visible throughout the entire sighting of the creature, which made good speed down the loch so easily, sometimes rising until some feet of black body could be seen. I felt that here was some unknown creature playing itself in Dores Bay . . . My brother-in-law began to talk of estimating distances but woman-like I was not interested. I was puzzled. I was almost shocked at what had happened to me. I kept repeating, 'What is it? It is black. It is big. It made a great speed leisurely. It must be – it can't be the Monster!' I was almost afraid to say the word aloud. Sightings are so rare that I had never expected that it would happen to me.

Miss Keith's brother-in-law, Mr James Ballantyne, wrote:

The head was completely similar to that of a python and was held at right angles to the neck. The neck was very elongated and slim, thickening at a point some one foot above the water. The neck and head stood some four to six feet above the water . . . I saw no body but the speed at which it went through the water with its head held high and the distance travelled could only make one surmise that it had a huge body and a very strong method of propulsion . . . it was perfectly silhouetted against the setting sun and I can only say that I have never been so fascinated and thrilled although it is also a trifle frightening.

On the evening of 18 July 1970 one of the animals was watched for several minutes in Urquhart Bay by Mr and Mrs John Tyrrel from Kenya, and Wing-Commander and Mrs Basil Cary, who live in a cottage on the southern side of the Bay. Mr Tyrrel, a lecturer at Nairobi University, told how 'I observed the object through my binoculars and saw several distinct wakes as it moved and a narrow sleekish neck which tapered only towards the end. It did not move continuously but in two or three surges.'

They stopped a passing car containing five people, and Wing-Commander and Mrs Cary came out of their house to see what the commotion was about. Mrs Cary takes up the story: 'By the time we got to the roadside there was just one hump visible, which looked dark brown except for where the light from the sunset was shining on it. After a moment it turned and went away towards the far shore and followed it for fifteen or twenty yards perhaps and then went down. But the nine of us stood and watched it, there was no question about it at all. The Tyrrels had had a marvellous view of the head and neck and body but the head and neck had gone down by the time we got there.'

In all, the Loch Ness Investigation Bureau accepted two hundred eye-witness accounts between 1963 and 1972, after a most rigorous pruning of all those which seemed at all doubtful.

The Fakers

Since a basic purpose of this book is to set the Loch Ness record straight it unfortunately becomes necessary to deal with those who have produced, wittingly or unwittingly, photographs which when scrutinized critically leave many serious doubts as to their authenticity. In approaching this most sensitive aspect of the story I have been strongly advised by many people simply to ignore these photographs. However, I feel that unless a clear distinction is drawn between reliable and unreliable evidence, the former can stand little chance of gaining credence and acceptance by the scientific community and the world at large. Fraudulent photographs infect genuine ones with the malignant reflux of suspicion; they confuse and degrade the real

124

issue for which so many people have been fighting for so long. It therefore seems correct to say a word about them since their continued production can only hinder scientific investigation of this subject.

On 2 October 1959 the *Sunday Express* reported that a twenty-six-year-old Gateshead fireman, Mr Peter O'Connor, was planning an expedition with sixty fellow members of the Northern Naturalists Association. The paper reported: 'The hunters will be armed with two Bren guns mounted on canoes, harpoon guns, underwater spearguns. "And," said Mr O'Connor, "we may use a bomb. I'll take a machete . . . if we are lucky we should only have one burst of firing." '

Mr O'Connor was speedily told by the authorities what he could do with his reported Bren guns and bomb, and the expedition was postponed. However, the following May, having appealed in vain to the Chancellors of the Universities of Oxford and Cambridge for help, Mr O'Connor went to the loch with one companion and camped near Foyers for a few days. At about 6.30 on the morning of 27 May, Mr O'Connor claims he took a photograph of one of the animals at a range of twenty-five yards whilst he was standing waist-deep in the water.

The photograph is truly amazing. It shows a large rounded body, sixteen feet long according to one of Mr O'Connor's estimates, and, to the front, a cylindrical object rising out of the water, which Mr O'Connor felt was the head and neck. In the *New Scientist* magazine of 23 January 1969, Dr Maurice Burton, who took a special interest in Mr O'Connor's photograph and had met him in 1959, wrote: 'On the shore (where Mr O'Connor claimed he had taken the picture a fortnight earlier) I found the remains of three large polythene bags, a ring of stones each about nine inches in diameter tied together with string and a stick that looked identical with the neck and head of O'Connor's monster. A photograph taken subsequently of an inflated polythene bag weighted with stones and with the stick wedged in front of it does not differ in any significant way from the O'Connor picture.'

Surprisingly, although it was two hours after dawn and the photograph was taken at water level, there is no background in the picture, just blackness. Mr O'Connor's stories, which together with his photograph have received quite wide publicity over the years, have contained so many contradictions that it would be unwise to accept this photograph as being a picture of one of the animals.

*

In August 1969, Mr Frank Searle settled at Loch Ness intent upon remaining there until he solved its mystery. His home was a small tent by the water's edge near Dores. For the first two and a half years of his continuing expedition, Mr Searle, a professional soldier for most of his life who before going north was the manager of a London greengrocery business, lived a hermit-like existence and maintained a constant and dedicated lochside vigil, enduring the many extreme hardships, both mental and physical, of full-time 'monster-hunting'. During this time he had only a simple box camera, and although he claimed to have made over a dozen sightings he did not take any photographs showing tangible or easily discernible objects.

In the summer of 1972 Mr Searle was loaned sophisticated cine camera equipment and bought a 35 mm. reflex camera with a 200 mm. telephoto lens. Since then, Mr Searle has produced and disseminated a number of sets of photographs which he claims show the unknown animals which inhabit Loch Ness. Despite the availability of cine cameras, he has never been able to shoot any cine film to corroborate his still photographs.

Of all Mr Searle's photographs, perhaps the most remarkable is a series which he claims (see the booklet *Loch Ness and The Great Glen*) to have taken on the early evening of 21 October 1972. According to press reports (*Daily Record*, various editions, 1 November 1972), he was out in his dinghy when 'there was a tremendous splash and the monster appeared.' He took a series of three shots of an object lying on the surface of the water showing a strangely ungraceful and disproportioned head and neck with a wide open mouth. In all three shots Mr Searle caught the 'animal' with its mouth open. The 'animal' then dived, according to Mr Searle, and reappeared a moment later on the other side of his dinghy, again about 250 yards away.

This time it was in a two-hump configuration – the smaller one purportedly being the head. The configuration does not change at all in the six further photographs he took. These photographs have been studied, and an unusually straight line has been observed on the back of the 'head' which, together with the sharp angle at the object's apex, gives it an appearance not unlike that of a floating oil-drum.

It is a regrettable fact which can be easily proved that these photographs have been tampered with. Mr Searle has also produced another series identical with the original shots in all respects except that an extra hump has been added to them by some process of superimposition or by rephotography.

Mr Searle also claims to have photographed the animals on 27 August 1972, 27 March and 1 August 1973, and 8 January 1974. All these pictures show curious shapes in the water very close to the beach. In all he claims to have over twenty photographs showing the animals.

Mr Searle's photographs have featured prominently in the popular British press and have been sold to newspapers, magazines and television companies throughout the world. Mr Searle has not, however, consented to the release of his pictures for serious study by photographic experts.

Because of the highly suspicious content of some of Mr Searle's photographs and the inconsistencies of the facts surrounding the taking of them, it is not possible to accept them as being authentic photographs of animate objects in Loch Ness. The true nature of the objects depicted in his photographs and the reasons for producing them are matters for speculation. A clue to the latter may lie in a remark made by Mr Searle when he was interviewed recently for an American television film (*Monsters – Mysteries or Myths?*, broadcast by CBS in November 1974). He commented: 'I figure it would be worth a lot of money; the use of the pictures by the media all over the world would fetch something like £200,000 over the first six months. After that there would be lectures, personal appearances and so on.'

So far the story has progressed from the day St Columba apparently saw a 'water monster' in Loch Ness in A.D. 565, through the centuries of Highland strife and upheaval into the modern era and the start of the 'monster-hunt' in 1933. Ever since the first watchers went to Loch Ness in the autumn of that year, the ambition has been to obtain a close-up photograph of one of the animals. Over the past forty years, several hundred thousand man-hours must have been devoted to this objective – without success. In the years immediately before 1972, successive expeditions did succeed in tracking large underwater objects on sonar but never managed to place a camera near enough to one of them to facilitate positive identification. These failures were about to be remedied.

In 1971, Dr Robert Rines and his Academy of Applied Science team brought an underwater electronic stroboscopic camera with them on their expedition. This equipment had been developed by Professor Harold Edgerton of the Massachusetts Institute of Technology – the famous 'Papa Flash' in Jacques Cousteau's adventures and inventor of the electronic flash-gun principle.

Although the strobe camera was operated without result over a two-week period in August 1971, earlier in the year Bob Rines did have the thrill of a surface sighting. Late in the long, light evening of 23 June, he, with his wife Carol and Wing-Commander and Mrs Basil Cary, observed a twenty-foot-long hump as it moved about two thirds of a mile away in Urquhart Bay. It was examined through a telescope from the Carys' cottage and compared in size to a fishing vessel anchored nearby. 'This', said Dr Rines, 'finally destroyed any last doubts I had that we are dealing with a very large living creature here at Loch Ness.'

*

The momentous 1972 season opened with yet another hoax – this time perpetrated by those who should have known better, a team from a Yorkshire zoo. On the last day of March they

128

publicly announced that they had found the body of a mysterious creature washed up near Foyers and that they had removed it and were taking it south for examination.

There are times when the establishment can act with amazing speed and this was one such occasion. Scotland's proprietary instincts were aroused, and police road-blocks were set up to foil this Sassenach plot to rob them of their 'Monster'. News-agency lines hummed, television news editors gasped, and Loch Ness residents sighed and remembered that tomorrow would be April Fool's Day. The hoax worked well until the police stopped the zoo men's van on the Forth road bridge, and the 'monster' was found to be a dead elephant-seal with its whiskers shorn off and its mouth padded out. The zoo 'scientists' did very nicely – a well-known Sunday newspaper splashed their 'How we fooled everybody' story all over its front page the next day.

That was the light side to 1972, the one which grabbed all the headlines and which has consequently been best remembered by the public.

At the beginning of August Bob Rines and a group from the Academy returned yet again with the underwater stroboscopic camera and Raytheon sonar equipment. In view of the important role which it was shortly to play, a word here about the construction of the stroboscopic camera. It consists of two water-tight cylinders, one of which contains a very bright flashing light; the other holds a 16 mm. camera which exposes one frame simultaneously with the light's illumination.

For several days a team consisting of the Academy scientists and Investigation Bureau volunteers operated the sonar and the camera without any response from the loch's depths. The research was concentrated in Urquhart Bay; every night, when the loch was quiet and deserted, they set out in two small boats and deployed the equipment in such a way that the area being photographed by the camera was monitored by the sonar.

Late on the evening of 7 August, the crews took up their positions as normal on the northern side of Urquhart Bay. The sonar transducer (the box which sends out and receives the signal) was lowered to a depth of about thirty-five feet from

129

the Bureau's boat *Narwhal*. About forty yards further out was the small motor cruiser *Nan*, from which the strobe camera was suspended at a depth of forty-five feet. The sonar beam was aligned to 'shine' in the direction of the underwater camera, which flashed and took a picture every fifteen seconds. Peter Davies of the Loch Ness Investigation Bureau, skipper of *Narwhal*, gave me this account of the night's events:

It had been quite choppy until about midnight, when the wind dropped and the water settled down to become jelly calm.

There were a lot of fish in the bay [salmon congregating for the autumn run up the river], which were appearing on the chart as tiny little dots about the size of a pin head . . .

It was about 1.45 a.m.; Hilary Ross was watching the sonar screen and Dave Wiseman and myself were drowsing. Hilary suddenly said that she thought something odd was coming on. We both got up and joined her and noticed that the fish dots were becoming streaks, as if the fish were all moving rapidly away from the area.

Then it started – a big, black trace started to appear. To begin with we thought it must be two or three fish close together. But then it got bigger and blacker and thicker; we could hardly believe our eyes – something huge was moving down there, very near to where the camera was. We watched it in silence for a moment – the size of it was so large in comparison with the fish. It appeared to be moving slowly but the trace kept on coming.

Peter then transferred from *Narwhal* into a smaller boat, *Fussy Hen*, tied up alongside, and started to paddle across to *Nan*, which held Bob Rines and the rest of the team.

I don't mind telling you that it was rather a strange feeling rowing across that pitch-black water knowing that there was a very large animal just thirty feet below. It was the sheer size of the echo-trace that was frightening. When I reached *Nan* I told Bob what was happening and he and Jan Willums [of the Academy] got into *Fussy Hen* and we rowed as quickly and as quietly as we could back across to *Narwhal*. When we got back on board the echo was still there, slowly being etched out on the paper. By now it was enormous, about the size of my thumb-nail. We were all excited but we just sat there, hardly daring to move, and watched in fascination and awe as the trace got longer and longer.

By now there were no fish at all on the screen – just the trace of whatever was beneath the boats. Peter went on:

Then a slight breeze got up and *Narwhal* started to swing round and we lost it. The trace stopped. I got out on deck and tried to paddle *Narwhal* round again with an oar but it was no good. It had gone.

Although nobody knew it at the time, the animal, since that is what was causing the echo, had been moving very near to the underwater camera and its picture had been taken. After forty long years of searching, one of these strange, elusive creatures had finally exposed itself to close-up photography. A series of pictures had been taken of its rear parts from a range of only twelve to fifteen feet.

A few days later, the Academy team flew back to America, taking with them the precious roll of 16 mm. colour film and the sonar chart in which were tied up the hopes of the entire Loch Ness investigation. Would this be the final solution?

The films were developed under bond at the head office of Eastman Kodak in the United States, whose staff signed statements that none of the films was tampered with in any way whatsoever. Among the reels shot during the expedition the sequence from the night of 7–8 August was located, and on this reel were four small frames showing the hazy outlines of something large and solid.

In order to improve the definition, spoilt by the gloom of the peat-stained water of Loch Ness, the pictures were sent to the American N.A.S.A computer-enhancement experts. This process has already been referred to in connection with the Surgeon's Photograph and Tim Dinsdale's film, but so that there can be no suspicion that the computer process fraudulently 'touches up' a picture it should be clearly stated that it merely improves clarity by electronically scanning a picture and, with the aid of filters, interpreting the missing or hazy portions by comparing adjacent grains.

One photograph in particular stands out: it shows a clearly recognizable flipper-like appendage joined to a roughly textured body. The hundreds of thousands of hours of searching were justified. Above all, it was the coincidence of the sonar and the photography which presented indisputable proof of the animal's presence. The one cross-checked with and corroborated the other. Here was the breakthrough.

During the next few weeks the photographs and the sonar chart were examined in secret by some of the world's leading authorities on sonar, photo-analysis and marine zoology. Their conclusions were cautious but displayed the muted excitement of scientists at last realizing that there really is a discovery – a tremendous discovery – to be made at Loch Ness. The photographic experts who measured the 'flipper' stated that it is about six to eight feet in length and two to four feet wide. In the frame taken fifteen seconds after the 'flipper-picture' a tail-like structure is visible which is measured as being 'at least eight feet long'.

Even our own British Museum of Natural History, which for so long shunned the Loch Ness question, had to sit up and take note. They examined the material in October at a secret meeting attended by Bob Rines and Tim Dinsdale and committed themselves to a public statement saying that there was no doubt that the photographs were genuine and that a large, moving object is visible in them. Dr J. G. Sheals, Keeper of Zoology at the Natural History Museum, stated, however, that '... information in the photographs is insufficient to enable identification.'

Members of the Smithsonian Institution, the principal scientific body in America, and the U.S. equivalent to the British Museum, were rather less circumspect. Professor G. R. Zug and Dr J. A. Peters stated that 'It has the shape of the tail of the palmate newt.' Mr H. Lyman of the New England Aquarium stated 'It does not appear mammalian. The general shape and form of the flipper does not fit anything known today.'

These few words from distinguished zoologists constituted the first small clues ever obtained to the identity of this species. At last the pieces of the jigsaw puzzle were beginning to collect.

When the sonar experts studied the chart evidence was found to suggest that a second animal was present when the photographs were taken. The length of the objects was estimated to be in the region of twenty to thirty feet (see the plate).

It is hardly necessary to point out the great significance of these results. They formed the first pieces of the irrefutable proof that has been sought ever since the 'Monster' first became an attraction and the first watchers went to the loch. As such they were and are of the most profound importance, both scientifically and for those who have dedicated themselves to the investigation of this mystery.

And yet, in spite of this, they received surprisingly little coverage when they were released in America by the Academy of Applied Science in November 1972. For some reason they were virtually ignored by the media – perhaps because the announcement coincided with the release of a set of highly suspect surface photographs which were splashed across the front page of a popular daily newspaper a few days earlier. Whatever the reason, the media gave only cursory references to the underwater material.

The scientific impact was, however, in inverse proportion to the public reaction, and in the summer of 1973 a more sophisticated research programme was launched by the Academy. A special underwater sonar triggering device, which responds automatically to the passage of any object larger than a predetermined size, was built by Dr Rines and his scientific colleagues and connected to a battery of underwater cameras and lights. The whole rig, valued at about £100,000, was set up in Urquhart Bay in July and operated continuously for three months. Not unexpectedly, after the tremendous success of 1972, the summer of 1973 drew a blank. No monstrous shapes ventured near the underwater apparatus, which, considering the very limited area of its coverage in the vastness of the loch, is hardly surprising. The creatures were not, even now, going to reveal their secrets easily.

The summer of 1973 also witnessed the first Japanese attempt at 'monster-hunting'. An enthusiastic oriental team arrived at the lochside in September, but regrettably their fervour was rather dampened when they realized the size of the task they had undertaken. The loch was not, as they believed, a small area with clear water, and after a couple of months of rather disillusioned sonar experimenting, the team left for what must have seemed the comparative sanity of their home country. Their sponsor, Tokyo impresario Mr Yoshio Kou, is now apparently considering which of several other 'great adventures' to investigate.

*

The Loch Ness investigation had reached a turning-point in its development. The Investigation Bureau closed down at the end of 1972 through lack of funds and of the necessary planning approval from Inverness-shire County Council to continue in occupation of its headquarters site. Despite its shortcomings it fulfilled, during its existence, the vital role of official overseer of the investigation. Although it failed in its intention of identifying the species inhabiting the loch, it did succeed in acting as an encouragement to others to pursue the search.

We have undoubtedly now come to the beginning of the end of the 'Monster' era. Now that real breakthroughs in the search are being achieved and the resources of modern science are being applied to the problem, it cannot be too long before the absorbing mystery of the identity of this strange species is finally solved and a new and very exciting animal is added to the order of zoology.

Chapter Eight

Monster Philosophy

Since taking his film in 1960, Tim Dinsdale has spent many thousands of hours searching for the answer to the mystery. Although he had brief head and neck sightings in both 1970 and 1971 he has not shot any more film. Such is the nature of this battle – for the time being success depends almost entirely on luck. Since he gave up his job in 1961 to devote himself more fully to the investigation, he has been on countless expeditions, exploring the loch both from the land and from boats. Recently I asked him what kept him going. This is the reply he gave:

Firstly because we are fighting for a matter of principle at Loch Ness – the truth, which is very important and is an absolute justification for the research.

Also, of course, I am intrigued by the mystery of it and by the fact that this business acts as a sort of mirror which reflects human behaviour. Our attitude to this sort of thing repeats itself, again and again. The scientific community, in particular, has behaved towards this just as it has always behaved towards things which are not readily explainable or understandable.

There are so many examples of science rejecting and vilifying subjects which it cannot understand or categorize. As a distinguished modern scientist, Professor Peter Medawar, writes: 'Scientists tend not to ask themselves questions until they can see the rudiments of an answer in their minds. Embarrassing questions tend to remain unasked and, if asked, to be answered rudely.'

The Loch Ness phenomenon has been an embarrassment to zoologists for the past forty years. Instead of facing up to it they have tended to turn their backs on the problem and in

135

some instances have tried to camouflage their inability to comment constructively by producing illogical statements without any reference to the real facts. Mr Philip Stalker, the first professional journalist to report on the 'Monster' way back in October 1933, and always one of the wisest journalistic writers on the subject, wrote in the *Weekly Scotsman* on 30 March 1957: 'If medical science had shown as little enterprise and as little courage, in its various fields, as marine zoologists have shown in regard to the Loch Ness animal, the Gold Coast would still be the White Man's Grave, appendicitis would still be a fatal illness and tuberculosis would be killing millions every year in Britain.'

The British Museum of Natural History made the following revealing comment about the affair in a booklet, *Scientific Research*, in 1956:

The most famous case of the unsubmitted specimen is that of the 'Loch Ness Monster', in which the ingenuity of suggestions as to the nature of the animal concerned has been equalled only by the powers of imagination of some observers. The only scientific evidence to which the Museum can point in explanation of this phenomenon is the report, published in the 'Glasgow Sunday Post' of 27th July, 1952, of some observations made by a theodolite by Mr Andrew McAfee. At a distance of 300 yards, he saw the three dark humps which characterize the description of the 'Monster'. With his theodolite, however, he was able to observe that the humps were shadows, and that they remained stationary while the ripples and wash of the water moved past them and gave the humps the appearance of movement.

The phenomenon would therefore be one of waves and water currents.

This statement typifies the shallow nature of the establishment's sense of impartial inquiry. Because they could prove that one apparent sighting was a mistake they felt justified in concluding that it represented the validity of all sightings. This same rather obsessive instinct to deal only with the material which can be explained away has recently been demonstrated by Dr Maurice Burton, formerly of the Natural History Museum.

136

In his book *The Elusive Monster* (Rupert Hart Davis, 1961), written after a week-long visit to the loch in 1960 which convinced him that the animals do not exist,* he tends to select those accounts which are doubtful and proceeds to pull them to pieces. When he comes to the Spicer land sighting he merely says: 'I found it difficult to believe this story also', and goes on to suggest that they saw a family of otters crossing the road. The otter is also, in Dr Burton's view, responsible for both the Surgeon's Photograph and Hugh Gray's, and is what Arthur Grant saw bounding across the road in front of him.

Bearing in mind that otters are only three to four feet in length such suggestions are patently absurd. Dr Burton's theories become even less impressive when one considers that until the end of 1959 he was arguing a diametrically opposite view. In the *Illustrated London News* of 20 February 1960 he wrote about the Surgeon's picture: 'If this photograph is genuine, as I am now convinced beyond all doubt it is, then there is no argument about the reality of the Loch Ness Monster, nor any doubt of its being a large animate body.' And in a letter dated 29 October 1959 he said: 'I have come to the conclusion that it is probably a plesiosaur-type animal.'

Perhaps a clue to Dr Burton's recent attitude lies in a remark he made in a letter dated 30 April 1962: 'I am now very resentful of those who, wittingly or unwittingly, have misled us and have caused me to spend so much time and effort needlessly, and to make me look ridiculous.'

Another of his dogmatic assertions is that Tim Dinsdale's film shows a boat, even though J.A.R.I.C., who actually studied the film, categorically state that it is no such thing. Despite repeated requests for a statement on the validity of the 1972 results Dr Burton has said nothing.

*

* Dr Burton described his inquiry as 'the biggest organised attempt to gather information on the problem of the Loch Ness Monster since the late Sir Edward Mountain took his team of observers north' (*Illustrated London News*, 16 July 1960).

I hope by now I have established that these animals do exist. What can they be? Since this book is intended to be a layman's history and not a scientific treatise, and in view of my personal lack of competence to argue scientifically on such matters, it would be impertinent and foolhardy for me to try to suggest the identity of a species about which so little is known. However, in order to complete the picture I can repeat what others, who are qualified, have said before or to me.

We can judge fairly accurately what the animals look like. From the hundreds of reliable eye-witness accounts and from the authenticated photographs an image emerges of a creature with a long, slender neck, small, 'snake-like' head, reasonably heavy body, a long, powerful tail and four apparently diamond-shaped paddles. Different witnesses have reported varying numbers of humps, from the one-humped 'upturned-boat' appearance to a two- or three-humped back. It has been suggested that this could be explained by a muscular flexing of the animal's body, possibly to assist in its propulsion. Alternatively, there may be some form of inflatable air-sac along the back which, when fully inflated, could appear as one hump (as in the Macnab photograph) and when deflated as two or three humps (as in the Stuart photograph). Such an air-sac might act like a ballast tank and would perhaps help the animals to submerge rapidly, as has been witnessed and determined from the sonar trackings.

The size of the animals seems to range from about fifteen to twenty feet to a maximum of perhaps fifty or so feet. The presence of a herd of the animals can reasonably account for most of the differences in size, colour and even overall shape reported by different witnesses. Little can be said about the structure of features on the head. Few observers have reported eyes or mouth, and no one, as far as I know, has reported seeing ears. However, on several occasions what have appeared to be snail-like stalks on the top of the head have been seen. Two witnesses who reported this were Mrs Greta Finlay and her son Harry, who in August 1952 were within about twenty yards of one of the animals near Aldourie Pier. Mrs Finlay described 'two six-inch-long projections from the top of the head, each with a blob on the end.' Could this be some form of retractable breathing apparatus, or perhaps even a distinguishing mark of one sex?

One of the most interesting sightings as far as head-detail is concerned took place in November 1973. The witness was Mr Richard Jenkyns, a retired farmer who lives with his wife in a house close to the water near Invermoriston. This is his account:

The date was Saturday, 10 November, and the time 11.45 a.m. The weather was stormy with a strong north-westerly wind and two-foot waves on the loch ;;; I was on the bank about ten yards from the shore and twenty feet above it.

I had just started a tractor with a loud bang when almost immediately I heard a very large splash, as if someone had gone in from the high board very flat . ;; I got off the tractor and went to look at the loch but could see nothing. A few moments later I glanced out again and there, nicely framed by a curved overhanging bough, about ten to fifteen yards out was a fish-like object (at first) starting to appear quite slowly and steadily until it was about eighteen inches above the water surface and then, a moment later, came up about another two feet. It then seemed to stay quite motionless for a short time and then moved slowly forward and slowly sank; It had travelled about forty yards;

Now, for the first time I realized that I had seen the beastie and I became rather bewildered. I could literally feel the hair on the back of my neck tingling;

Its colour was black or browny grey, texture neither rough nor smooth or shiny; matt is the best word I can think of; Diameter about nine inches, no fins or gills. There appeared to be very large scales on the head, but this was only an impression. There was a great gash of a mouth at least nine inches long and tight shut, and above the centre of the mouth what may have been a small, black eye or a blow hole ;;; the general appearance was that of a tube, slightly rounded at the top with the head profile rather like that of a snake.

How did the animals get into the loch? There are two possibilities: either the species has been trapped in it for several thousand years or it has entered more recently. When the last Ice-Age ended, about 10,000 years ago, the ice melted and the level of the sea was raised, flooding many coastal valleys until the land, freed of the weight of ice, slowly rose and separated the sea from the inland waters. J. B. Sissons in *The Evolution of Scotland's Scenery* (Oliver and Boyd, 1967) explains it thus: 'The sea overtook the slowly rising land and invaded the coastal areas of much of Scotland, extending far inland along the major valleys.'

It is possible that, during this period when Loch Ness was linked to the sea, a group of these animals swam into its sheltered waters and settled there. Eventually they found their return route to the sea blocked as the land rose and Loch Ness became an enclosed lake. Slowly the water lost its saline content, and the animals adapted to their new freshwater existence (a change which has been accomplished successfully by many other species; there are sharks in freshwater lakes in parts of Africa which were once connected to the sea).

The only alternative is that a family has entered the loch at some time since its isolation from the sea. Since Loch Ness is fifty-two feet above sea-level the possibility of an underground tunnel can be ruled out. The only other potential entrance is via the River Ness, running from the loch's northern end into the sea at Inverness. However, this river is usually quite shallow, and it seems unlikely that a family of even young animals would attempt to ascend it from the sea.

The fact that the loch is about fifty feet above sea level also more or less rules out any possible links with other Highland lochs. That this species exists in other lakes, notably Loch Morar (where many similar sightings have been reported and which was investigated recently by the Loch Morar Survey Group), is undeniable but it is not possible that the animals commute from one home to another.

And so just what is this 'modern phoenix', as Constance Whyte put it? Are they mammal, reptile, amphibian, mollusc, fish or something which does not fit into any of these categories?

One must first consider what we know of their breathing habits. The scarcity of surface appearances suggests that they are not mammalian, since if they were they would need to come

140

to the surface to breathe. It is, however, just possible that they have nostrils set high on the head so that they need expose only this part of the body when breathing. In August 1934 Count Bentick, his wife and their daughter from Holland (his sister was lady-in-waiting to the Dutch Queen) were at the Halfway House, Altsaigh, when they saw the top of the animal's head just protruding above the surface. From its mouth, Count Bentick noticed, 'a kind of steam came forth, but was blown back by a slight cold breeze.' This account would seem to support the surface-breathing theory but, in isolation, it is not possible to attach too much importance to its implications.

Of all the candidates for the identity of the 'Monster', the most widely canvassed is undoubtedly the plesiosaur – a marine, fish-eating dinosaur thought to have been extinct for about seventy million years. This is a theory which was put forward by Dr Denys Tucker, the former British Museum expert mentioned in Chapter 7. If this is correct it would undoubtedly make the discovery the greatest zoological find of recent centuries. And indeed it must rate as a very distinct possibility, since one of the plesiosaur family, the elasmosaurus, was, as far as can be judged from skeletal remains, virtually identical in appearance to the animals in Loch Ness. It had the same long, slender neck, small head, long tail and four flippers and it is known originally to have existed in the area of the British Isles.

The discovery of an animal thought to have been extinct for millions of years has, of course, a precedent. In 1938 a coelacanth, a five-foot-long, steel-blue-coloured fish thought to have been extinct for sixty to seventy million years, was caught by a fishing boat near Madagascar. By the time it was examined by Professor J. L. B. Smith of Rhodes University, the carcase had almost rotted away. However, enough remained to convince him that this was a coelacanth, an animal which he believed to be a missing link in the development of fish and amphibian reptiles.

Another specimen was not caught for fourteen years, not until December 1952 when a native on the Comoro Islands landed one on a fishing line. Professor Smith was vindicated and

141

his colleagues were forced to gape in astonishment. He wrote at the time: 'Why is this discovery so important? It is a stern warning to scientists not to be too dogmatic . . .'

It is a hard lesson to teach; it is one that was not absorbed after the discovery of other zoological 'impossibilities' such as the giant squid at the end of the nineteenth century and which has still not been learnt today.

Professor Roy Mackal, one of the directors of the old Loch Ness Investigation Bureau and a Professor of Biochemistry at the University of Chicago, has made a close study of all the possible identities of the animals. The results of this study are to be published in his book *The Search at Loch Ness*, but he has kindly allowed his conclusions to be mentioned here. This is what he told me:

It is by no means impossible that we have a plesiosaur here, but there are two other theories which I prefer, having gone through the entire animal kingdom and compared the data we have gathered at Loch Ness to all the possible species which might fit.

My first choice would be some evolutionary derivative of a primitive aquatic amphibian of a species called the embolomer, which was found in the Carboniferous period about 270 million years ago. Alternatively, and rather less exciting, we could have a very large, thick-bodied eel-type creature here.

At the very least it will be a very great discovery at Loch Ness, whatever they turn out to be.

The amphibian theory has, of course, received support from some of the analysts of the 1972 underwater pictures, who pointed out a similarity between parts of the photographed objects and parts of a 'palmate newt'. An amphibian, that is, some form of newt or salamander, would seem to fit very well, since it can live happily in water or on land and can breathe through its skin.

The trouble with drawing a comparison between the animals in Loch Ness today and those which are known to have existed millions of years ago is that, during those millions of years, a creature could have evolved into a different shape and have developed new fundamental structuring. Whatever is in Loch Ness may well be an embolomer or a plesiosaur which has slowly changed in response to the peculiar requirements of existence in a very dark, cold freshwater loch.

Although dinosaurs are believed to have been cold-blooded and could therefore not live easily in cold water,* nature has a remarkable facility for fashioning animals which can survive in what may, to a mind perhaps rather befuddled by scientific theory, seem an impossible or unlikely environment.

Fish, apart from the eel, seem a very unlikely contender in view of the animals' distinct neck and the fact that they apparently exceed the maximum theoretical size of any gilled creature. Lastly, the invertebrate theory rather falls down when the land sightings are considered, since a creature of this bulk would appear to need a backbone and skeleton in order to transport its body on land. The only other possibility is that Loch Ness harbours something entirely unknown – a species not related to any of the known orders of animal. Whatever they are, they must have their ancestry in the sea, which naturally leads to some form of link with the legendary sea-serpent.

Throughout this book I have referred collectively to 'animals' in Loch Ness. This is contrary to the rather widespread belief that if there is a 'Monster' it must be one solitary, superannuated and probably rather senile individual. This has never been seriously suggested as a possibility. Several sightings of two creatures have already been described here, and there are more which could be listed.

For instance, on 13 July 1950 a party of eight people watched three of the animals swimming about 300 yards out in the loch. One of the witnesses was Mr R. R. Gourlay. He described to the *Daily Express* what happened: 'In the centre were two black, shiny humps, five feet long and protruding two feet out of the water. On either side was a smaller monster, one of which made a great splashing noise as it disappeared towards the opposite shore. The largest monster and the small one travelled together towards Urquhart Castle.'

In 1972 an American scientific journal, *Limnology and Oceanography* (Vol. 17, No. 5), published a short article en-

---

* Recent research has, however, suggested that some of them may have been warm-blooded.

titled 'The Population Density of Monsters in Loch Ness', by R. W. Sheldon of the Fisheries Research Board of Canada and S. R. Kerr of the Bedford Institute of Oceanography. Working on theoretical figures for the standing stock of the fish population and 'logarithmic size intervals' they concluded: 'A viable population could be quite small but probably would not be less than ten ... It seems therefore that Loch Ness must contain a small number of large monsters. These could weigh as much as 1,500 kg. with a population of 10 to 20 individuals. A 1,500 kg. monster could be about 8 m. long (approx. 22 feet), a size that agrees well with observational data.'

Are these creatures dangerous? Evidence indicates that they are basically timid, but their very size and bulk require that they be respected. The reader may recall Alex Campbell's experience of having his boat heave under him as if something was surfacing from below. And, as many witnesses will testify, it is a very shocking, if not rather frightening experience to see one of these animals. The reason is quite simple; at Loch Ness one is dealing with the unknown, with an animal which, because of its size, has an inherent ability to inspire awe and wonder.

There are two locally quite well known stories of men actually being overcome by the sight of the animals. One day during the First World War a Mr James Cameron, head gamekeeper at a local estate, went into the Drumnadrochit Inn, his face as white as paper, and asked for brandy. He refused to say what had happened, but later he did tell a friend, Mr Kenneth Mackay, of how he had been out fishing in Urquhart Bay when an 'enormous animal' had surfaced close to the craft. The next thing he remembered was coming round, lying in the bottom of the boat.

On another occasion, this time going back to the year 1889, a Mr H. J. Craig and his brother were fishing from a boat near Urquhart Castle. Suddenly 'a huge form reared itself out of the water and went off at great speed.' In a letter to the *Inverness Courier* of 27 September 1947, Mr Craig wrote that he and his brother rowed for the shore in a state bordering on hysteria. When their father heard their story he instructed them never to tell anyone or refer to the incident again.

Fish have several times been seen to react to the presence of one of these animals. Mrs Winifred Cary, who had her first sighting in 1917 when she was a child, describes how in July 1954 she saw a big hump coming across the loch, '... and as it came nearer I saw salmon leaping out of its path and the thing seemed to turn and follow the fish.' And on one Sunday morning in June 1969, when the loch was very calm, '... suddenly, in a strip about thirty or so yards long by about fifteen to twenty yards wide I saw fish moving everywhere and rising and jumping right out of the water, and yet they weren't rising anywhere else on the loch. And then through the middle of the fish I saw a wash going along towards Temple Pier, and a moment later a hump appeared at the head of the wash.'

Of the habits of the animals we know little. The only thing that can be said with certainty is that they are not primarily surface dwellers and they are certainly not inquisitive – if they were, they would have been located many years ago. The sonar research done by Bob Love in 1969 and 1970, consisting of numerous end-to-end sweeps of the loch, covering about 55 per cent of the water area, suggested that the animals are bottom- and side-dwelling. More than that it is impossible, at the moment, to say.

It is, of course, their almost total elusiveness which accounts for the lack of photographic proof of their existence. Despite the tens of thousands of hours of surface observation by hundreds of 'monster-hunters' the results have been depressingly meagre.* It is hard fully to appreciate the problems of the investigation without having visited Loch Ness and experienced the frustration of weeks or months of watching without any result. Large as these animals are, they have an enormous area

* There are, however, said to be two cine films of the animals in Loch Ness which have never been seen because they are locked up in a bank vault. Both were taken in the 1930s, one reputedly by a Dr MacRae at a range of only one hundred yards and the other by a London banker, Mr James Currie, who spent ten days looking for the animals in 1938 and was rewarded with a film of the head, neck and humps. So far it has been impossible to locate these films or even verify their existence. Mr Currie's film is said to be legally locked away 'until such time as the public takes such matters seriously.'

in which to hide and very little inclination to expose themselves to the groups of anxious aspiring photographers. When one is seen, unless the viewer has a powerful camera and the presence of mind to use it, it can usually escape without giving anything away. Once one chance has gone it could be months or, as in Tim Dinsdale's case, years before another opportunity arises.

People frequently ask why, if the animals exist, are no carcases ever washed up? The answer is, as the local saying goes, that 'the loch never gives up its dead', because of its great depth and very low temperature. When a body expires it just settles on the bottom and is slowly covered by mud and silt. Given time and resources, it ought to be possible either to dredge the bottom or inspect it by submarine and locate the remains of one of the animals.

*

It is sometimes suggested by writers from Fleet Street and elsewhere that people who look for 'Monsters' in Loch Ness are a community of romantic drop-outs – a peculiar by-product of the irreverent and ungodly twentieth century, who are sustained by an addictive need to worship the bizarre. Certainly, many of those who have taken part in the investigation have been inspired by a quixotic enthusiasm and a renegade desire to give the establishment a sharp kick in the pants but, in every case I can think of, such emotions have always been tempered by a rational and carefully conceived belief in the reality of the animals. Above all, it has been the certain knowledge that one day they must be proved right that has kept successive generations of monster-hunters going; the belief that tomorrow, next month or next year the shred of final evidence must be forthcoming and all the immeasurable physical effort thereby justified. It is a belief that has remained undiminished as summers have closed every year for nearly half a century.

And it is a belief which now, in the autumn of 1975, appears to be on the brink of fulfilment.

Postscript: September 1975

The Solution

No one will ever understand Loch Ness. Its conquest will be a greater triumph than the conquest of the moon.*

Just before 7 o'clock on the evening of Friday 29 August 1975 the telephone at my home in Leeds rang. An American voice inquired: 'Mr Nick Witchell? Transatlantic call for you from the United States.' After a short pause Bob Rines came on the line to announce news that meant the search for the 'Monster' of Loch Ness was finally over. 'Nick,' his voice came clearly and steadily over the thousands of miles, 'we've got it, we've hit the jackpot. We have detailed close-up colour photographs of the head, neck and body of one of the animals.'

He went on to describe how the latest batch of underwater photographs, taken back in June, had just been received from the Eastman Kodak laboratories where they had been devéloped under strict security conditions. In one shot, he told me, was a colour close-up of the head of the animal, showing the mouth and what appeared to be breathing tubes; in another the neck, fore flippers and part of the body could be seen. The jackpot indeed.

*

A few days later, on 3 September, I flew to America to view the material. Later that night Bob and his wife Carol welcomed me to their apartment overlooking Boston Harbour. In due course the room was darkened, a white window blind was lowered to act as a screen, and Bob pulled a small paper packet of slides from his trouser pocket.

* A British journalist writing in the *Daily Express*, 4 July 1961.

The first picture he projected showed the hull of a boat, photographed from underneath. Bob explained that it had been taken immediately before one of the pictures of the animal, when the camera had evidently been swirled around so violently that it had been tilted upwards and had photographed the underside of the boat from which it was suspended by a rope line.

At this point I should explain that these pictures were all taken with the old Edgerton underwater strobe camera, not with the main automatic rig as I had assumed from Bob's telephone message. The Edgerton camera, designed and built by the famous 'Doc' at the nearby Massachusetts Institute of Technology, was the old 'warhorse' piece of equipment which had photographed the 'flipper' back in 1972. Bob went on to describe how at about 4.30 p.m. on the afternoon of 19 June he had lowered the Edgerton camera (a motor-driven 16 mm still camera and a bright strobe light, each in a separate cylinder, which fire simultaneously) from the Academy boat *Hunter*, moored in Urquhart Bay, simply as an auxiliary camera.

The Edgerton was suspended on a rope line to a depth of forty-five feet. Forty feet below it, sitting on the floor of the loch, was the main, automatic camera rig, which was linked to the sonar triggering device. The Edgerton camera cylinder and the accompanying light cylinder were both lashed to a tubular frame and were held in such a way that they were pointing slightly upwards as they hung freely suspended in the water. They had been set to take a picture every seventy-five seconds; the camera was loaded with ordinary High Speed Ektachrome colour reversal film.

Suddenly the slide changed: the picture of the boat hull had gone. In its place was a much darker image with, in the upper left corner, the body of an animal with a very long, outstretched neck, gliding down towards the camera.

Everyone carries with him clear recollections of moments so vivid, so striking that they will never, however long and turbulent the passage of time, be erased from his memory. For me this was one such moment. I have never seen the animals of Loch Ness, despite having spent many months at the loch and

148

many tens of thousands of hours watching for a surface appearance. During the summer of 1972 I spent five months living in a small wooden hut which I built in a field overlooking Urquhart Bay and filled with powerful cameras; the following year I spent three months there: all without success so far as a sighting was concerned.

Therefore to look at this photograph in the certain knowledge that it was the most complete picture ever taken of one of the creatures was a truly awe-inspiring experience. The animal was facing almost head-on to the camera. Beneath the body were two clearly definable appendages. The skin looked very rough and potted, even at this range (which had been estimated at thirty to forty feet), and was a red-brown colour.

Bob flicked on to an enlargement of the body. The most striking feature was the length of the neck column, no doubt accentuated by the angle of the photography. It stretched in an arc across the picture and appeared to fade away at its end. At once, phrases used by eye witnesses came to mind: the head which could not be distinguished from the neck and merely looked like a continuation of it; here it was, exactly as it had been described.

I had stood up to move closer to the screen and remained there as Bob moved to the next slide. The picture that came on to the screen was, without doubt, and I make no apology for the continued use of superlatives, the most remarkable animal photograph ever taken.

It was the head of the creature, in close-up detail from a range of only eight feet. For a few seconds the shapes were a tangle; then it suddenly fitted together. The head occupied the left-hand section of the frame and was more or less in profile: the open mouth of the animal showed what appeared to be teeth inside it; a prominent, bony ridge ran down the centre of the face into a thick, hard-looking upper lip; two nostril shaped marks were situated above the upper lip, one on either side of the central ridge. Most remarkable of all, there were two clearly defined stalks or tubes protruding from the top of the head.

Bob had warned that the head was ugly. 'Gargoyle' was the word he had used and he was most certainly right. It was hideous: angular, bony and revolting. Again, eye-witness accounts came to mind; without exception, witnesses who had been close to the head had stressed how very ugly it was and there was no difficulty in understanding why, looking at the face of the beast.

Over the years I have been involved in the Loch Ness saga I have on innumerable occasions wondered how it would end; what form the final, conclusive evidence would take. Until Bob Rines initiated the use of underwater cameras it had always been assumed that a film of one of the animals on the surface would eventually be the clinching proof. I don't think anybody believed that a picture such as this would be the end-product of this epic search. To have captured so much facial detail would be impossible with an above-water camera; this one shot demonstrated the futility of the surface photography mode.

Underwater photography had always been dismissed as impossible because of the murkiness of the water in Loch Ness. Admittedly, of course, Bob Rines had access to the best underwater photographic expertise in the world, that of Professor Harold Edgerton at MIT, but if this type of research had been used from the beginning the animals would have been discovered years ago. As it was, Rines had achieved in four years what all other investigations had failed to do in over forty.

The light from the strobe had caught the beast in the mouth; the interior was clearly illuminated and much lighter than the dark browny colour of the remainder of the head. The light had also caught the tops of the two stalks on the top of the head. Their presence made me think of one eye-witness report in particular, that of Greta Finlay in 1952 (see pp. 138–9). She had described two horn-like projections on the top of the head, as have others from time to time.

The final good picture showed the underbelly of the animal as it passed immediately above the camera. A cylindrical object stretched across the whole frame. The most noticeable feature of this was the covering of what were evidently parasites hanging off the belly.

As we went through the whole sequence of pictures again, Bob described the reaction of a group of experts from the

Smithsonian Institution who had flown over from Washington the previous day to see the pictures. Headed by Professor George Zug, the head of the Reptiles and Amphibians Department, they had been utterly amazed at what they had seen. They had, he said, noticed details which only the trained zoological eye would see; for instance on the underbelly picture they had been particularly interested by the parasites and there had been speculation that a dark area towards the left end could be the creature's anal fold.

Afterwards Bob produced a set of sketches he had obtained from the Zoology Department of Harvard University. They showed skulls and skeletons of the ancient plesiosaur – the marine dinosaur believed to have become extinct seventy million odd years ago in the latter part of the Cretaceous period.

I have already stated that when approaching the problems of identification it is quite wrong for an untrained person such as myself to attempt to offer theories about the classification of the creatures. All I will say is that looking at the sketches of fossilized remains of the plesiosaurs it was impossible not to be struck by the resemblance. The head in the photograph had the same bony ridge down the centre of its face, the same large mouth and nostrils set in the same place as the skulls in the sketches. In addition, the fossilized skulls appeared to show sockets on the top of the head to correspond with the stalks on the top of the animal's head.

It has been suspected for years that in general outline the Loch Ness animals may resemble the plesiosaurs. In 1972 the 'flipper' picture established that they have fins identical in structure; now the portrait of the head revealed features which again appeared to fit the theory. It will, of course, be for the experts from the Smithsonian Institution and the British Museum to put a name to the animals, and perhaps the 1975 pictures will be insufficient for positive classification. They do, however, point the way most powerfully towards one sensational conclusion.

Next morning I prepared a short cable to Constance Whyte, who I knew would be waiting anxiously for news at her home in Sussex. 'Amazing picture of horrific head. Greta Finlay was

151

correct. Smithsonian very excited' it read. Dictating it to the cable operator I felt sorry that there were not more people from Britain to share in the viewing of the pictures. So many should have been present: Constance Whyte, Tim Dinsdale, David James and scores of others who have devoted so much to the investigation.

Later I lunched with Bob Needleman, Executive Director of the Academy of Applied Science and one of the participants in their Loch Ness programme. He told me how they had all more or less given up hope of any success with the underwater films they had brought back from Loch Ness after their June experiments until, on a casual examination of the reels from the Edgerton camera, the pictures had been discovered.

The reels which they thought might have contained something had come from the automatic camera rig, which had been triggered by the sonar sensors for ninety-two seconds and forty-five seconds on 27 and 29 June respectively. It was the news of these two incidents that had leaked out to the press in July and had given rise to the speculative stories which appeared at that time. However, when these films, which were an extremely light-sensitive black-and-white variety, were developed they were found to be completely washed out: the film had been too sensitive and was no good.

'We thought we'd flunked out again,' remarked Bob. 'All we had left were the colour films from Doc's [Edgerton's] camera.' When these were returned from Kodak, complete with signed affidavits from the technicians who had processed them, testifying that they had not been tampered with in any way and that they were completely normal underwater exposures in every respect, they had remained unexamined for over a week. Bob Needleman explained: 'To view the pictures from the Edgerton camera we have to project them through a 16 mm time-lapse projector and it took a few days to get one and to set everything up.'

The man who carried out the first, shattering examination of the film and who thereby became the first person ever to see the 'Monster' in such detail was Charles Wyckoff, President of Applied Photo Sciences of Needham Heights, Boston, one of the

152

most active members of the Academy team and a former member of America's nuclear science programme. 'I reckon to have seen some pretty weird things in my time,' he told me later, 'but nothing matches what I saw that evening when I went through that film.' He described how he had been flicking through the frames, projecting them on the time-lapse projector, when, at frame 438, the shot of the underbelly appeared on the screen. 'I couldn't make it out. It reminded me at first of a shot of the bottom of the ocean, there were so many small objects covering the main expanse of it.'

With his curiosity keenly aroused, Charlie proceeded flicking through the film. Blank picture after blank picture appeared on the screen until, at frame 726, the shot of the animal gliding down towards the camera came on. 'This really made me sit up, but I was still unsure and so went on very quickly.' There was nothing else for a further 300 frames or more. Then, at frame 1069, the picture of the underside of the boat appeared. Two frames further on and the head flashed on to the screen. ' "Holy crow", I thought, "that looks like a cabbage".' Obviously the animal had closed in on the camera and had either knocked it with part of its body or swirled the water so violently that the camera was tilted up and took a picture of the boat's hull. Then, two frames later, with the animal's head only about eight feet away and looking almost directly at the lens, it had snapped again and destroyed the creatures' centuries-old anonymity.

The picture of the boat hull is, in fact, a most valuable bonus, since it provides a ready-made calibration; the hull is twenty-four feet in length and it is approximately forty-five feet away. With the knowledge of the strobe beam's ability to penetrate the murky water the task of measuring the dimensions of the objects photographed becomes comparatively simple.

The pictures were all taken on 20 June: the first in the series, the underbelly, in the early morning, probably at about 9 o'clock; the neck and body shot at about midday, and the head picture later in the afternoon. These times are interesting since they indicate that the animal (if, indeed, it is the same one in all three pictures) was passing the camera at regular intervals. It is quite possible that it was attracted by the rhythmic flashing of the strobe light and returned each time to investigate this strange intruder into its territory. The open mouth in the head picture suggests that it was possibly trying to attack the camera, but Bob Needleman assured me that there were no scratch marks on the cylinder when it had been pulled up at about 4.30 p.m. on the afternoon of 20 June.

The next problem was to decide what to do with the pictures. Obviously the first step would be to submit them for confidential study to the zoological authorities of Britain and America and then, in due course, to release them to the world. Already the Academy had been approached, on the strength of the previous month's rumours, by newspapers and magazines with offers for any pictures. However, the need for extreme caution was obvious; little would be gained by an immediate announcement to the press; the material had first to be analysed and ratified by the appropriate authorities.

On the final day of my visit to Boston the Editor-in-Chief and two senior executives from the *National Geographic Magazine* flew over from Washington to meet Bob Rines and discuss arrangements for the publication of the pictures. At Charlie Wyckoff's laboratory the photographs were projected. 'Jesus Christ – look at that,' exclaimed Gilbert Grosvenor, great-grandson of the *National Geographic*'s founder, Alexander Graham Bell, and now its Editor-in-Chief, as the body and neck picture appeared on the screen.

It was fascinating to see their reaction. Here were three shrewd outsiders, with no commitment to either the Academy or Loch Ness and whose attitude to the pictures was bound to be hyper-suspicious and critical. Immediately they were gripped with the same excitement that the rest of us had been going through for the past few days or weeks.

Whatever the result of these negotiations, the likelihood is that some at least of Dr Rines's pictures will have been published to the world towards the end of this year. By then the material will have been examined by a team of experts led by Dr John Sheals, Keeper of Zoology at the British Museum, whose responsibility it will be to ratify the discovery of the animals. It is hoped that a verbal presentation cum press conference will be held in Edinburgh immediately after the pictures have been published, attended by representatives of the British Museum together with spokesmen for Inverness-shire and the national government. It will be their vital responsibility to warn the inevitable hordes of bounty-hunters that any interference with the animals will not be tolerated.

*

With the official ratification of the discovery of the animals in Loch Ness, the world will lose one of its most popular mysteries: the Loch Ness Monster. There will be many who mourn the passing of 'Nessie'; she has been a pleasant distraction during her forty-odd years of existence, consistently playing with aplomb the role of a genial pea-brained brute that popped up from a haze of alcoholic fumes on those 'Phew What a Scorcher' summer days when nobody wanted to think very seriously about anything.

However, as the one mystery dies it is replaced with another, of even greater proportions. It is the mystery of how these very large animals, whether they be marine dinosaurs or not, have survived in isolation and seclusion in such a populous part of the world for so long. Their discovery contributes considerably to man's sum total of knowledge about the world in which he lives, and for that reason alone the efforts to discover them can surely be totally justified.

Tempting though it is, it would be invidious now to gloat and pour too much scorn on the scientific establishment for its attitude to Loch Ness. Scientists have a duty to be sceptical and to demand the firmest evidence before accepting anything which claims to be a new contribution to knowledge. What is inexcusable is the scorn they themselves have poured on the testimony of sober and reliable witnesses in the course of several decades and their refusal to follow it up with any serious investigation, a refusal entirely in line with the unfortunate scientific tradition of rejecting any discovery which fits none of the convenient pigeon-holes of the time and thus upsets a comfortably tidy picture of the world. The discovery of the Loch Ness creatures is the triumphant conclusion of a quest conducted almost entirely by amateurs, moving against the official tide of opinion to achieve what must be one of the most important natural discoveries of this century.

The moral of the Loch Ness story is simple. It points to the value of retaining an open mind. Science would benefit considerably if it could drop some of its academic arrogance and listen respectfully to the testimony of intelligent but scientifically untrained observers; the media would serve their audiences better if they paid more attention to the sober consideration of facts rather than to glib, uninformed, instant judgements and flippant headlines.

The world still holds many mysteries awaiting solution by those with inquiring minds and a sense of adventure. Loch Ness itself still hides many secrets, which will doubtless begin to unfold as more sophisticated research programmes get under way. Britain now finds herself the fortunate custodian of one of the world's most remarkable gifts of Nature. Whether the nation deserves such luck in view of the way it has treated the affair is questionable, but it is now absolutely essential that steps be taken at the highest levels to protect these animals from the unscrupulous, who will inevitably try to plunder and exploit the discovery.

These animals are one of the greatest wonders of the world. Let us, in the name of reason and decency, make absolutely certain that they continue to enjoy what legend has it they were once granted by St Columba – the everlasting freedom of the loch.

More about Penguins
and Pelicans

The Goshawk

T. H. White

Stories of close relationships between men and beasts –
Born Free or *Ring of Bright Water* – possess peculiar
fascination. To this T. H. White added an individuality of
style and independence of philosophy which makes *The
Goshawk* a classic of its kind. As David Garnett has
written: '*The Goshawk* is the story of a concentrated duel
between Mr White and a great beautiful hawk during the
training of the latter – the record of an intense clash of
wills in which the pride and endurance of the wild raptor
are worn down and broken by the almost insane willpower
of the schoolmaster falconer. It is comic; it is tragic; it is
all absorbing. It is strangely like some of the
eighteenth-century stories of seduction.'

'Mr White impregnates every sentence with the fire of
passion and mellows it with the tenderness of affection. I
rank *The Goshawk* as a masterpiece' – Guy Ramsey in the
Daily Telegraph

Not for sale in the U.S.A. or Canada

The Soul of the White Ant

Eugène Marais

Is nature a state of chaos or a predetermined pattern of existence? Is a termite colony a collection of individuals or a single, unified organism working towards a single aim?

In this utterly absorbing study of a termite colony, Eugène Marais, the brilliant South African journalist, lawyer, poet and natural scientist, poses these intriguing questions. Ten years of close observation led him to some startling conclusions – with disturbing social implications.

'As a scientist he was unique, supreme in his time, yet a worker in a science yet unborn' – Robert Ardrey

Not for sale in the U.S.A. or Canada

The Year of the Seal

Victor B. Scheffer

In this book Victor Scheffer, who won the John Burroughs
Medal with *The Year of the Whale*, again skilfully
combines fiction with fact to give an imaginative and
absorbing account of a year in the life of an Alaska fur
seal.

Drawing on scientific research in the Pribilof Islands and
inspired by a deep love of his subject, he traces a Golden
Seal's life patterns and shows how she is uniquely adapted
to function on land and in the sea.

The Year of the Seal is a fascinating guide for the layman
and a 'must' for all those interested in this graceful
animal.

The Year of the Whale

Victor B. Scheffer

To date very little is known about the leviathan of the
deep – an animal which man has ruthlessly hunted to
virtual extinction.

In *The Year of the Whale* (winner of the John Burroughs
Medal), Victor Scheffer brilliantly combines scientific
documentation with imaginative reconstruction to present
a detailed and absorbing account of the first year in the
life of a sperm whale.

This is a reliable and informative introduction to the study
of the whale which provides fascinating insights into the
habits of the grandest of all mammals.

Not for sale in the U.S.A. or Canada

Gavin Maxwell in Penguins

Ring of Bright Water

'A small masterpiece, all who read this beautiful book will see life in new colours' – *Books and Bookmen*

'Engrossing and magnificent' – *Spectator*

'A masterpiece . . .' – *Listener*

The House of Elrig

This is the personal story of Gavin Maxwell's childhood and boyhood, most of which he spent, in fact or in fancy, at the House of Elrig, a lonely, windswept house on the moorlands of Galloway. This is the house which, together with the influence of his relations, shaped his interest in living creatures and his love of wild country and wildernesses, and led to the way of life he describes so brilliantly in *Ring of Bright Water*. Few books have described with such vividness the impact of the countryside on a sensitive child, and its power to enrich and sustain.

'The finest piece of writing Mr Maxwell has yet produced' – *Sunday Times*

Not for sale in the U.S.A.

Gavin Maxwell in Penguins

The Rocks Remain

Ring of Bright Water described the pioneering days at Gavin Maxwell's lonely cottage on the West Highland seaboard with the otters Mijbil and Teko. *The Rocks Remain* the story of the succeeding years is a further superb evocation of a personality, a place and a way of life – though it is not without its disastrous episodes.

The author records his sojourns in North Africa, throwing into vivid contrasts his joyful returns to Camusfèarna, where the warmth and friendship and his close contact with the otters remains an integral part of the story.

'As beautifully written, as vivid and as moving as its predecessor' – *Guardian*

Not for sale in the U.S.A.